W9-AKU-071

Editor
Gisela Lee

Managing Editor
Karen J. Goldfluss, M.S. Ed.

Editor-in-Chief
Sharon Coan, M.S. Ed.

Cover Art
Lesley Palmer

Illustrator
Renée Christine Yates

Art Coordinator
Kevin Barnes

Art Director
CJae Froshay

Imaging
Temo Parra

Product Manager
Phil Garcia

Publishers
Rachelle Cracchiolo, M.S. Ed.
Mary Dupuy Smith, M.S. Ed.

Authors

Jane Carroll Routte and Ann Greenman Barnell

Teacher Created Materials, Inc.

6421 Industry Way
Westminster, CA 92683
www.teachercreated.com

ISBN-0-7439-3630-2

©2002 Teacher Created Materials, Inc.
Made in U.S.A.

Table of Contents

Welcome to Canada

Canada is a land of great variety. This country is the second largest country in the world in terms of land area. Within the boundaries of this huge land are many interesting people, places, and traditions. Canada is the home of the world's largest shopping mall, the world's largest Easter egg, and the world's tallest free-standing tower. One-third of the world's fresh water supply lies within the boundaries of Canada. Canada has large cities and small villages. It is a land of varied traditions and interesting history.

Canada's Maritime provinces border the Atlantic, and their rugged coasts attract visitors from all over the world. The French traditions of Quebec give that province a unique flavor in the new world and offer traditions and experiences unlike anywhere else in North America. The industrialized areas of Ontario are home to the largest populations in Canada and produce the majority of manufactured goods in the country. The Great Plains of Saskatchewan and Manitoba are the bread basket of Canada and supply wheat to the world. Alberta's breathtaking scenery makes the Rocky Mountain wonderland the destination for campers, canoers, and hikers from all over the world. British Columbia's mountains beautiful access to the Pacific make this most western province a center of commerce and tourism. The territories of the Yukon and the Northwest territories preserve large expanses of the most untouched natural land in the world, and they contain huge deposits of natural resources and varied wildlife. Nunavit, Canada's newest territory, is home to the Inuit people and is important in preserving that group's traditions and way of life.

Canada's history is filled with excitement and diversity. French and British colonization made a huge impact on the nation. Although Canada is an independent nation, it is still considered part of the British Commonwealth, and the Queen of England is considered sovereign. Many people of Quebec still owe allegiance to their French heritage, and this issue has maintained the French language. Votes for Quebec to become a separate French-speaking nation have been narrowly defeated in recent years and have caused strife among various political factions in the country.

Welcome to Canada *(cont.)*

Other groups have also influenced the growth of Canada. As in the United States, many immigrants from Europe and other parts of the world came to Canada seeking a better life and personal freedom. German, Ukrainian, Polish, Italian, Japanese, and Chinese people have made their homes in Canada for generations, largely influencing the culture of the country. Recent newcomers from Mexico, Southeast Asia, and India are adding to the cultural diversity of Canada today.

The native people of Canada have many long-honored traditions in the country. The amazing artistry of the west coast people with their signature totem poles and wooden masks is a hallmark of native artwork. The creative stone carvings of the Inuit and the etchings on whalebone and walrus tusks display the human need for creativity even in the harshest of climates. The ability of the native people to survive Arctic winters is a testament to human strength, endurance, and creativity. The tribes of the mountains and plains share many of the traditions of the Native Americans of the United States, and the stories of their struggles to maintain their traditions and way of life is similar, too.

Canada's diversity makes it a wonderful land to explore and study. Students will never run out of amazing things to find out about Canada. The amazing Niagara Falls, the beauty of the Rocky Mountains, the diversity of wildlife, and the dinosaur digs of Alberta, all of these will add to the excitement that students can find about Canada. Interesting crafts and exciting chuck wagon races are side-by-side with the Royal Canadian Mounted Police and the Klondike Gold Rush.

History, cultures, geography, science, language, and math all come together in the study of this country. You and your students will enjoy the journey across Canada. Activities in this book have been classroom tested and are carefully chosen to help the busy teacher. It is recommended that you use the Provincial Fair as your culminating activity, as it gives the class a chance to bring many of their projects and experiences together. It also provides an opportunity for the students to demonstrate their knowledge to other students, parents, and the community. However you choose to use this book, we know that your students will develop a life-long interest in the fascinating country of Canada.

4

Canadian Almanac

Here is some general information about Canada that will help you understand more about this wonderful country.

Size: 9,970,610 sq. km/3,849,653 sq. mi. This makes Canada second only to Russia in area.

Coastline: 250,000 km/155,350 miles (Six times around the equator!)

Border with the U.S.: 8,892 km/5,513 miles (The longest undefended border in the world!)

Largest Island: Baffin Island 388,500 sq. km/150,000 sq. mi.

Largest Lake: Great Bear Lake 32,652 sq. km/12,607 sq. mi.

Largest River: River Mackenzie 2,635 km/4,241 mi.

Highest Mountain: Mount Logan 6,050 m/19,850 ft.

Canada grows one-third of the world's wheat and has one-third of the world's fresh water supply.

There are ten provinces (Alberta, British Columbia, Manitoba, New Brunswick, Newfoundland, Nova Scotia, Ontario, Prince Edward Island, Quebec, Saskatchewan) and three territories (the Northwest Territories, Nunavit, and the Yukon)

National Capital: Ottawa, Ontario

There are 38 national parks (with plans for several more).

The largest is Wood Buffalo in Alberta and the Northwest Territories. This park has the largest herd of free-range bison in the world and is the only nesting site in the world for the endangered whooping crane.

Average Life Expectancy: 76.1 years for men and 81.8 years for women

Coldest Official Temperature Ever Recorded: -63°C/-81°F in 1947 in the Yukon

Canada covers seven time zones, although Yukon Standard time is usually replaced with Pacific Standard Time.

Resources on the Internet

These sites have interesting information about Canada, the people, and the traditions. There are many more sites with helpful information, and new ones are constantly developing. Use your Web browsers to find more.

http://www.calgarystampede.com (get a western nickname)

http://www.stampedeagriculture.com

http://www.bcchs.com/ (British Columbia Cowboy Heritage Society)

http://www.cowboylife.com/index.html (general information about cowboys in Canada and elsewhere)

http://www.iaw.com/~falls/ (comprehensive site for Niagara Falls information)

http://www.kids.premier.gov.on.ca/ (Ontario)

http://collections.ic.gc.ca/flag/ (flag)

http://collections.ic.gc.ca/index.html (index of general Canadian information)

http://www.crwflags.com/fotw/flags/ca.html (flag information)

http://www.stcum.qc.ca/ (Montreal Metro)

http://www.tyrrellmuseum.com/bshale/ (dinosaurs and fossils)

http://www.tyrrellmuseum.com/index.htm (dinosaurs)

http://www.albertapaleo.org/ (dinosaurs)

http://www.canadapolitics.about.com/cs/capitalcities/

http://www.canadaonline.about.com

http://www.vancouver.hm/canfacts.html (great source of Canadian facts)

Resources on the Internet *(cont.)*

http://www.ucdsb.on.ca/links/gov.htm (government and education links)

http://www.gov.nu.ca/ (Nunavit government)

http://www.vegreville.com/tp2.html (world's largest Easter egg facts)

http://www.pysanka.com/ (pysanka eggs)

http://www.dmc.nmc.edu/arctic_spirit/accS046.html (Inuit art)

http://www.culturel.org/NUNAVUT/ (Inuit sculpture)

http://www.inuitart.org/ (Inuit sculpture)

http://collections.ic.gc.ca (Inuit sculpture)

http://www.eclatart.com/Inuit_Art_Gallery_Enter.html. (Inuit sculpture)

http://www.mala.bc.ca/www/discover/educate/posters/lauriec.htm (Kwakiutl masks)

http://projects.edtech.sandi.net/kimbrough/kwakiutl/ (lesson about Kwakiutl indians)

http://www.oakislandtreasure.com/

http://ag.arizona.edu/tree/drm/recipes/nanaimo.html (Nanaimo Bars)

http://www.capcan.ca/faq/index_e.html (Ottawa – World's longest skating rink)

http://www.canada.trav.net/ontario.html

http://www.evergreen-washelli.com/text/totem_poles.html (totem poles)

http://www.washington.edu/burkemuseum/nwtotem.html (totem poles)

http://www.mnh.si.edu/arctic/index.html (Arctic studies)

http://www.mnh.si.edu/arctic/html/sea_mammals.html (Arctic animals)

http://www.nhl.com/ (official site for the National Hockey League)

http://www.carnaval.qc.ca/index.htm (winter carnaval in Quebec)

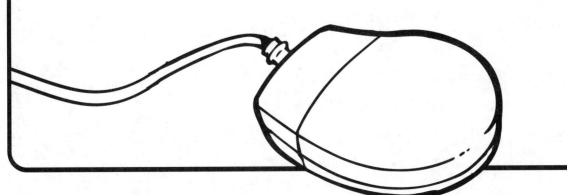

Bibliography

Ansary, Mir Tamim. *Arctic Peoples*. Heinemann Library, 2000.

Bakken, Edna. *Alberta*. Grolier, 1991.

Barlas, Robert. *Welcome to Canada*. Gareth Stevens Publishing, 1999.

Barlas, Robert. *Canada*. Gareth Stevens Publishing, 1998.

Barnes, Michael. *Ontario*. Lerner Publications, 1995.

Berton, Pierre. *Pierre Berton's Canada*. Stoddart, 1999.

Bowers, Vivien. *British Columbia*. Lerner Publicatins, 1995.

Bowers, Vivien. *Wow, Canada!: Exploring This Land from Coast to Coast*. Owl Books, 1999.

Campbell, Kumari. *Prince Edward Island*. Lerner Publications Co., 1996.

Campbell, Kumari. *New Brunswick*. Lerner Publications Co., 1996.

Coates, Helen R. *The American Festival Guide*. Omnigraphics, 1998.

Costa, Vincenzo. *Dinosaur Safari Guide*. Dinosaur Safari Guide. Voyageur Press, 1994.

Culin, Stewart. *Games of the North American Indians*. University of Nebraska Press, 1992.

Dabovich, Lydia. *The Polar Bear Son: An Inuit Tale*. Clarion Books, 1997.

Dahl, Michael S. *Canada*. Bridgestone Books, 1998.

Daitch, Richard W. *Northwest Territories*. Lerner Publications Co., 1996.

Drake, Jane. *Forestry*. Kids Can Press, 1996.

Eber, Dorothy. *Pictures Out of My Life*. University of Washington Press, 1972.

Emmond, Kenneth. *Manitoba*. Grolier, 1991.

Grann, Marjorie. *New Brunswick*. Grolier, 1995.

George, Jean Craighead. *Arctic Son*. Hyperion Books for Children, 1997.

Hamilton, Janice. *Canada*. Carolrhoda Books, 1999.

Hamilton, Janice. *A Ticket to Canada*. Carolrhoda Books, 1999.

Hamilton, Janice. *Quebec*. Lerner Publications Co., 1996.

Hancock, Lyn. *Northwest Territories*. Grolier, 1992.

Hancock, Lyn. *Yukon*. Lerner Publications Co., 1996.

Harrison, Ted. *O Canada*. Ticknor & Fields, 1993.

Houston, James. *Confessions of an Igloo Dweller*. Houghton Mifflin, 1996.

Indians of the Northwest. Gareth Stevens Publishing, 1997.

Joose, Barbara M. *Mama, Do You Love Me?* Chronicle Books, 1991.

Bibliography *(cont.)*

Kessler, Deirdre. *Prince Edward Island.* Grolier, 1992.

Landau, Elaine. *Canada.* Children's Press, 1999.

LeVert, Suzanne. *Alberta.* Chelsea House Publishers, 1991.

_____. Chelsea House Publishers, 1991.

_____. *Manitoba.* Chelsea House Publishers, 1991.

_____. *Newfoundland.* Chelsea House Publishers, 1992.

_____. *Nova Scotia.* Chelsea House Publishers, 1992.

_____. *Ontario.* Chelsea House Publishers, 1991.

_____. *Prince Edward Island.* Chelsea House Publishers, 1991.

_____. *Quebec.* Chelsea House Publishers, 1991.

_____. *Saskatchewan.* Chelsea House Publishers, 1991.

_____. *Yukon.* Chelsea House Publishers, 1992.

Lotz, Jim. *Nova Scotia.* Groiler, 1991.

MacKay, Katherine. *Ontario.* Groiler, 1991.

Margoshes, Dave. *Saskatchewan.* Groiler, 1992.

Murdoch, David. *Cowboy.* Alfred Knopf, 1993.

Murdoch, David. *North American Indian.* Alfred A. Knopf, 1995.

Nanook of the North. Kino Video, 1992.

Nanton, Isabel. *British Columbia.* Groiler, 1994.

Nickles, Greg. *Canada.* Raintree-Steck-Vaughn Publishers, 2000.

Quellet, Danielle. *Quebec.* Groiler, 1993.

Ray, Delia. *Gold! The Klondike Adventure.* Lodestar Books, 1989.

RCMP: The March Camp. GAPC Entertainment, Inc. 1999.

Rogers, Barbara Radcliffe. *Canada.* Children's Press, 2000.

Schemenauer, Elma. *Canada.* Child's World, 1998.

Shepherd, Donna Walsh. *Klondike Gold Rush.* Franklin Watts, 1998.

Sylvester, John. *Canada.* Raintree Steck-Vaughn, 1996.

Thomson, Ruth. *The Inuit.* Children's Press, 1996.

Wyatt, Gary. *Spirit Faces: Contemporary Native American Masks from the Northwest.* Chronicle Books, 1995.

Yates, Sarah. *Manitoba.* Lerner Publications, 1996.

M Is for Maple

M is for Maple by Michael Ulmer is a wonderful picture book that makes an excellent introduction to Canada. The book is in an alphabetical format and covers everything from *Anne of Green Gables* to zippers (which were perfected in Canada).

Use the book as a beginning activity. Have the children discuss the variety of things mentioned in the book. Explain to them that Canada is a very large country with many interesting people, places, and events.

Before reading the book, ask students what they already know about Canada. After reading the story to them, have them tell you what they learned. Which things about Canada surprised them?

The book is a good starting point for other activities in this book. You can also use it to spark interest in report topics.

When the class is finished with the Canada unit, they can make their own alphabet book of Canada using different ideas for each letter of the alphabet. Each student could be assigned a letter to do, and the class can come up with a book of its own.

Have students write four-line poems about things that they learn as they complete the unit. At the end, make a Canadian poetry book.

As you read the book, have the students listen for these things.

- What important women were mentioned?
- Who were some of the important men mentioned?
- Which person mentioned do you think was most heroic?
- Why are islands important in Canada?
- Why was the book called *M is for Maple*?
- How many national parks are there in Canada?
- What do you think is the most interesting thing in the book?
- Which thing in the book would you like to learn more about?

Famous People from Canada

Canada has been home to many famous people. Canadians are successful in all fields. Medicine, inventing, sports, music, art, and entertainment are just some of the fields where Canadian citizens have reached fame and success.

Here is a list of famous people from Canada. Read the list and find out how many you recognize. Choose one of these people and read more about him or her. Use the My Famous Canadian Report form to write a report to share with your classmates.

Ned Hanlan (1855–1908): world champion Toronto rower

James Naismith (1861–1939): invented the sport of basketball in 1891

Tom Longboat (1887–1949): marathon runner

Barbara Ann Scott (1928–): figure skater

Marilyn Bell (1937–): long-distance swimmer

Wayne Gretzky (1961–): hockey player

Pauline Johnson (1861–1913): one of Canada's best known poets in the 1890s and early 1900s; she was born on the Six Nations reserve near Brantford, Ontario

Joe Shuster (1914–1992): Toronto cartoonist; he co-created *Superman*, the comic book hero, in 1938

Glenn Gould (1932–1982): internationally-famous concert pianist, recording artist, and composer

Karen Kain (1951–): ballerina

Dan Aykroyd (1952–): actor, writer, and comedian

Jim Carrey (1962–): comedian and film star

Alanis Morissette (1974–): singer/songwriter

John McIntosh (1777–1846): started apple growing on a large scale

Daniel Massey (1789–1856): started the most successful farm machinery company in the British Empire

Famous People from Canada *(cont.)*

Alexander Graham Bell (1847–1922): invented the telephone between 1874 and 1876

Sir William Osler (1849–1919): called "the most influential physician in history"

Sir Frederick Grant Banting (1891–1941): physician, physiologist, and Nobel Prize winner for insulin

Joseph Brant (1742–1807): Mohawk chief, scholar, statesman, and soldier. He fostered relationships between the British and American and the Iroquois Confederacy.

Roberta Lynn Bondar (1945–): first Canadian woman in space

Jay Silverheels (Harry Jay Smith) (1919–1980): actor who played Tonto on "The Lone Ranger"

Marisu Barbeau (1883–1969) : Quebec-born Canada's most famous folklorist

Madame Benoit (1904–1987) : chef

Margot Kidder (1948–): actress

Bryan Adams (1959–) singer

Kim Campbell (1947–) : first woman prime minister

Emily Carr (1871–1945) : artist

Leslie Nielsen (1926–) : actor

John Candy (1950–1994): actor

Shania Twain (1965–) : singer

Celine Dion (1968–): singer

Buffy Sainte-Marie (1941–) : musician, composer

Joni Mitchell (1943–) : musician, composer

Kenojuak Ashevak (1927–) : artist

Michael J. Fox (1961–) : actor

Terry Fox (1958–1981) : raised money for cancer research by organizing and training for the Marathon of Hope, a run across Canada; he inspired the Terry Fox Run in Canada

David Suzuki (1936–) : scientist, writer, radio, and TV host

Donald Sutherland (1934–) : actor

There are many, many more famous people in Canada. Investigate some of these or others. You will be surprised how many people you have heard about come from Canada.

My Famous Canadian Report

My name is _____

The person I chose to report about is _____

I chose this person because _____

_____

_____

_____

_____

_____

My person is famous because _____

_____

_____

_____

_____

_____

_____

What I learned about my person _____

_____

_____

_____

_____

_____

I used these sources to find out about my famous person _____

_____

_____

_____

_____

My Famous Canadian Report *(cont.)*

If I could spend a day with my famous person, I would want to ask him or her these questions

_____

_____

_____

_____

_____

_____

If we spent a day together, I would like to go to and do these things together _____

_____

_____

_____

_____

_____

_____

The most interesting thing I learned about my person is _____

_____

_____

_____

_____

_____

_____

Geography and Science

Map Projects

Maps are excellent projects to display around the classroom. Three-dimensional maps bring to life the actual physical characteristics of an area. These map projects will help your students visualize the country of Canada and its topography.

Here are two map-making projects which you may choose to use in your classroom.

Using a black outline map of Canada (see page 18), project the map onto a large sheet of white paper on a wall for the students to trace. After the outlines of the country and provinces are traced, have the students write in the names of the provinces and their capitals. Students may want to color in the provinces in the manner of a political map. Use the list provided on the next page for this activity.

Have the students make topographical maps using a recipe of flour, salt, and water to make a dough mixture. Project the geographical regions map on a large piece of cardboard and have the students mark the geographical features of Canada. Use the dough mixture to form the shape of Canada, its mountains, and plains. This map may take some time to dry properly. Have the students paint the various geographical areas in different colors. Small flags can be glued to toothpicks and stuck into the map to show important cities and places of interest.

Ingredients

- salt
- water
- flour

- food coloring
- newspaper or sheet of plastic to protect the work surface

Directions

1. Mix one part flour with one part salt.

2. Stir in water until mixture is thick but not too wet. The mixture should be the consistency of clay and should be able to be molded in to mountains. You may add food coloring to the mixture at this point.

3. Allow this type of map sufficient time to dry; it may take one or two days depending upon the humidity. You may paint the map after it is dry.

Provinces, Territories and Capitals of Canada

Canada is the second largest country in the world. This very large country is divided into sections called provinces and territories. Canada has ten provinces and three territories. Each province and territory has its own capital, and Canada has a national capital in Ottawa, Ontario. Here is a list of the provinces and territories and their capitals. They are listed by how they rank in population. Notice that some of the largest areas have the fewest people. Why would that be true?

Province/Territory	Capital
1. Ontario	Toronto
2. Quebec	Quebec City
3. British Columbia	Victoria
4. Alberta	Edmonton
5. Manitoba	Winnipeg
6. Saskatchewan	Regina
7. Nova Scotia	Halifax
8. New Brunswick	Fredericton
9. Newfoundland and Labrador	St. John's
10. Prince Edward Island	Charlottetown
11. Northwest Territory	Yellowknife
12. Yukon	Whitehorse
13. Nunavit	Iqaluit

Color in the provinces on the map on the next page.

Number each province with the correct number from the list above.

Locate the capital for each province and put a star where it is.

Map of Canada

18

Map of Canada Answer Key

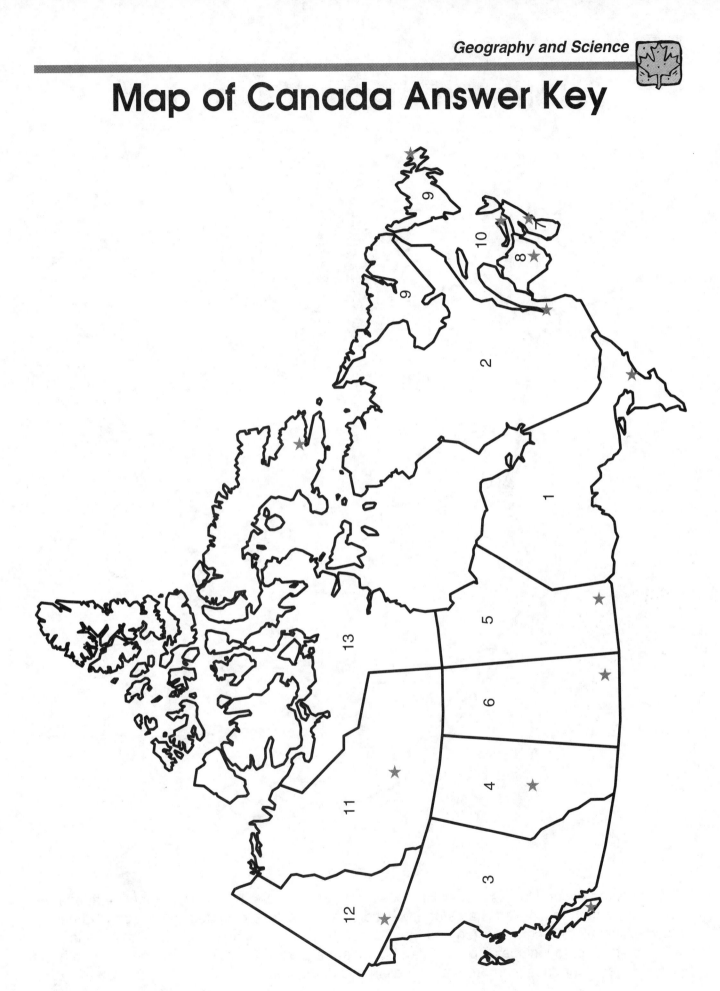

North American Countries

Canada is the second largest country in the world. You can see by this map that Canada is much larger than the United States and Mexico. Color the United States brown (don't forget to include Alaska!) and color Mexico and the Central American countries yellow. Color Canada red. Don't forget to include all of the islands that are a part of Canada. Now you can see how much bigger Canada is than other countries in this hemisphere.

A Two-month Night?

To help your students understand the long winter night and the long summer day of the Arctic North, read *Arctic Son* by Jean Craighead George.

The Land of the Midnight Sun is the name given to the Arctic regions near the North Pole. From November 20 until January 20, the Arctic regions see no sun. In the summer from May 10 until August 3, the sun does not set. The length of this day and night cycle changes according to the line of latitude from which it is observed.

Use the following experiment to explain to your students how the day and night can be so long at the North Pole.

You will need a globe and a flashlight. Give the flashlight to one of the children who will represent the sun.

Set the globe on a table. Show the students that the earth's axis is not straight up and down.

Stand so that the North Pole is away from you. Shine the flashlight on the Tropic of Capricorn. This is where the sun hits the earth on December 21. Spin the globe and notice that the sun does not hit the North Pole. You will have to adjust the distance that the "sun" stands from the globe based on the size of the globe.

Now have the "sun" move to the other side of the globe so that the North Pole is tilted toward him or her. Shine the light on the Tropic of Cancer. This is where the sun is on June 21. Spin the globe. Notice that the North Pole is always in the sun. This is the "Land of the Midnight Sun."

Have the children experiment with moving around the globe. Explain to them that this is what causes us to have seasons. Have them observe what happens at other locations on the globe. Notice how the length of the day changes all over the globe as the sun moves from place to place. Be sure to explain to the children that in reality, the earth is moving and the sun is stationary.

The students should be familiar with the following terms:

rotation—the earth's turning on its axis

revolution—the earth's making one pass on its orbit around the sun

equator—zero degrees latitude

Tropic of Cancer—the line of latitude 23 degrees and 27 minutes north of the equator

Tropic of Capricorn–the line of latitude 23 degrees and 27 minutes south of the equator

North Pole—the northernmost point on the earth

A Two-month Night? *(cont.)*

Can you imagine a day when the sun doesn't shine at all? How about a night when the sun never sets? Both of these things happen near the North Pole. Watch as your teacher shows you how the lengths of the days changes with the seasons. Use this page to record what you learn.

Label the lines on each diagram. Find the North and South Poles.

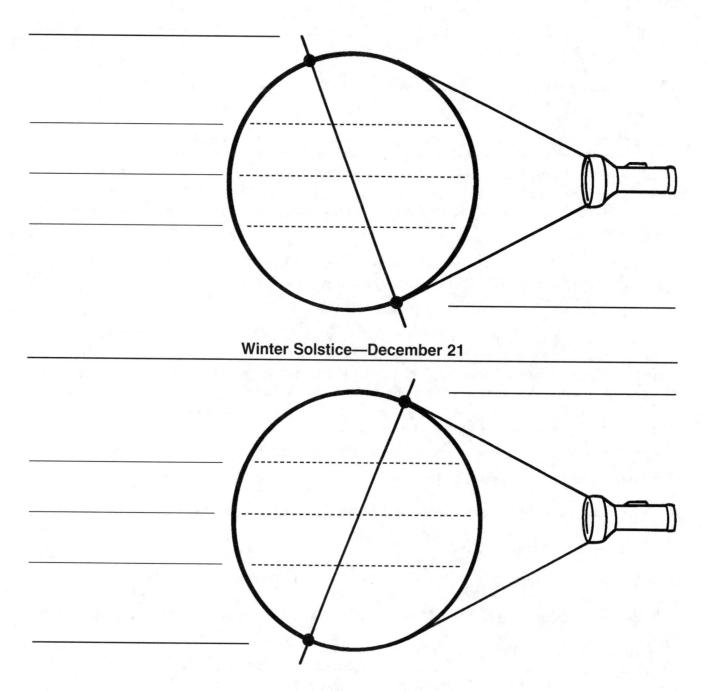

Winter Solstice—December 21

Summer Solstice—June 21

It's About Time

Canada has six time zones. The time zones are Pacific, Mountain, Central, Eastern, Atlantic, and Newfoundland. The difference between the time in Newfoundland and British Columbia is only 4.5 hours. Much of Canada observes Daylight Savings Time, but some places choose not to use it. The Island of Newfoundland has its own time zone that is one-half hour different from Atlantic Time. There is also a Yukon Time Zone, but it is not used much anymore.

Time zones all over the world are measured from Greenwich Mean Time (GMT). The Newfoundland time zone is 3 ½ hours behind GMT. The Atlantic zone is 4 hours behind GMT. The Eastern is 5 hours behind. The Central is 6 hours behind. The Mountain is 7 hours behind. The Pacific is 8 hours behind.

Look at the map on the next page and answer the questions below.

1. It is 1:00 Atlantic time. Draw hands on the clock at the top of the map on page 24 to show the correct time in each time zone.

2. You are in New Brunswick. Your sister lives in Alberta. You told her you would call her at 5:00 P.M. on her time. What time would it be at your house when you place the call?

   _____

3. You get on a train in Manitoba at noon. It takes two hours for the train to arrive in International Falls, Ontario. What time would it be in Ontario when you arrive?

   _____

4. You cross the border from Quebec to Ontario. Will there be a time change for you?

   _____

5. You go from Alberta directly north to the Northwest territories. Will there be a time change for you?_____

6. You are on Prince Edward Island, and it is 9:00 A.M. You call a friend in Newfoundland. What time will it be for your friend?_____

7. How many time zones will you pass through if you travel from Nova Scotia to British Columbia?_____

8. Which time zone would you be in if you were standing on the eastern shore of the Hudson Bay?_____

9. If you go from Alberta to Ontario, how many time zones would you go through?

   _____

10. Will the time zones get wider or narrower as you travel north? Why?

    _____

Hint: Fold this section under before reproducing.

Answers: 1. The clocks should read: Newfoundland 1:30, Atlantic 1:00, Eastern 12:00, Central 11:00, Mountain 10:00, Pacific 9:00 **2.** 8:00 P.M. **3.** 1:00 P.M. **4.** no **5.** no **6.** 9:30 A.M. **7.** three (that you pass through) **8.** Eastern **9.** one **10.** narrower because the lines of longitude get closer together near the North Pole

Canada's Time Zones

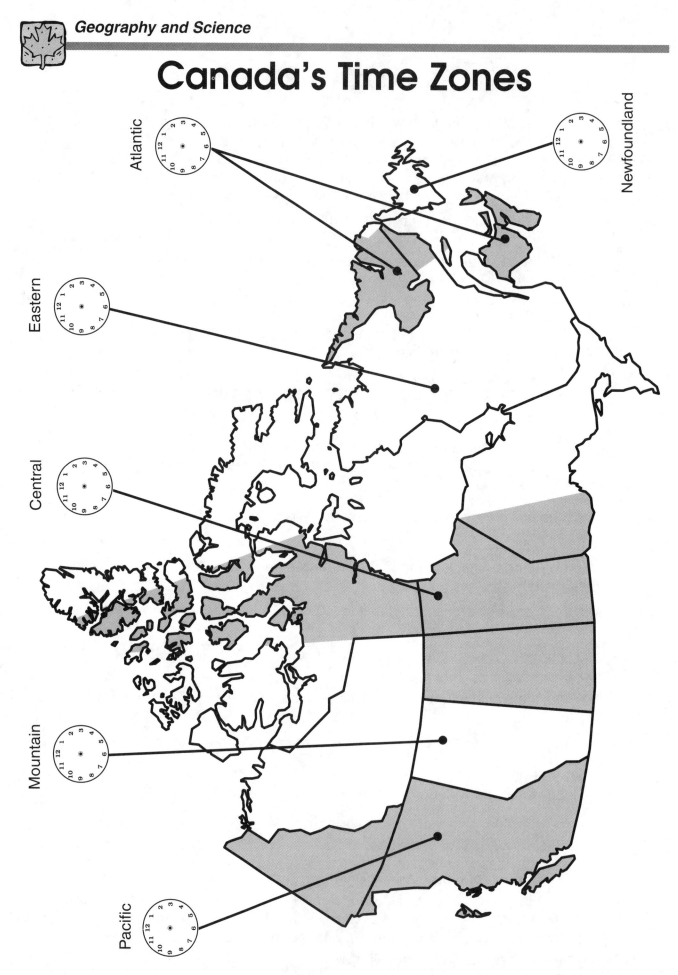

24

Niagara Falls

Background Information

Niagara Falls is one of the most famous falls in the world. The small falls belong to the United States and are called The American Falls and the Luna Falls, sometimes called the Bridal Veil Falls. The larger Horseshoe Falls is in Canada.

Niagara Falls is a popular tourist site, and for many years it has been particularly known as a honeymoon spot. People from all over the world come to see the falls, and as you walk around the area, you can hear people speaking many different languages.

The first European to announce the existence of Niagara Falls was Father Louis Hennepin, a Franciscan Friar who was traveling with French explorers, in 1678. He greatly exaggerated the size of the falls, but he was correct about hearing their roar 45 miles away. The Iroquoian word *niagara* means "thunder of water." The native tribes believed that one of their gods, Hinu, lived behind the falls and made the great noise.

In 1678 the falls were very different from what they are now. The falls were further north on the river, and they were not as horseshoe-shaped as they are today. As the land eroded under the falls, they moved south and formed the wider falls that we see today.

Niagara Falls is on the Niagara River, which actually flows from south to north. This river is the link between Lake Erie and Lake Ontario. Lake Ontario is 332.5 feet (101 meters) lower than Lake Erie. Niagara Falls connects the upper level of the Niagara River to the lower level. Although Niagara Falls is not the highest falls in North America (Yosemite Falls, California, is 739 meters or 2,424 feet), it is the most powerful, with the largest volume of water speeding over it each day.

If you visit the falls, you can get very close to them in two ways. One way is to go "under the falls." There are tunnels on the Canadian side that take visitors to an observation point right up next to the water. Another way is to take "The Maid of the Mist," a boat which carries passengers close to the foot of the falls. Either way, you have to wear a raincoat because you'll get soaked!

Niagara Facts

The American Falls (including Luna or Bridal Veil Falls) 1,100 feet (335 meters) wide 180 feet (55 meters) tall 38,000 tons (34,200 metric tons) of water per minute goes over these falls
The Canadian Falls (Horseshoe Falls) 2,500 feet (762 meters) wide 170 feet (52 meters) tall 342,000 tons (307,800 metric tons) of water per minute goes over these falls

Niagara Falls Daredevils

Niagara Falls has always attracted people who wanted to challenge the power of the falls. These people wanted to prove that they could survive going over the falls or walking above them on tightropes. Here is a list of the people who have challenged Niagara Falls. You might want to find out more about these people and write a report on them.

1829	Sam Patch	He dived into the falls from Goat Island.
1859–1860	"Blondin" Jean Francois Gravelet	He walked across the top of the falls on a tightrope many times, sometimes carrying other people on his back!
1860	"Signor Farini" William Hunt	He challenged Blondin by also walking a tightrope and trying to do more dramatic walks than Blondin.
1876	Maria Spelterini	The first woman to walk across the river on a tightrope. Crossed several times.
1892	Clifford Claverley	Tightrope walker. Sat on a chair in the middle of the rope and read the newspaper.
1901	Annie Edson Taylor	The first person to go over the falls in a barrel and live. She is the only woman who has ever gone over the falls alone.
1911	"Great Houdini" Oscar Williams, not the famous Harry Houdini	Tried to cross a tight wire by hanging with his teeth, but he was not successful and had to be rescued.
1911	Bobby Leach	Went over in a steel barrel.
1925	Charles G. Stephens	Went over in a barrel, and all they ever found was his tattooed arm!
1928	Jean A. Lussier	Went over in a large, hard rubber ball supported by steel ribs. He survived.
1930	Gene Strathakis	Went over in a barrel and got trapped behind the wall of water. He died of suffocation, but his barrel and his pet turtle survived.

26

Niagara Falls Daredevils *(cont.)*

1951	William Hill, Jr.	Went over in a contraption called "The Thing," which was made of automobile inner tubes. He died.
1961	"Nathan Boya" William Fitzgerald	Went over the falls in a scientifically engineered ball of rubber and steel. He was the first person to be arrested for going over the falls.
1984	Karel Soucek	Went over in a barrel. He was fined $500.
1985	Steven Trotter	Went over in a cylinder. Fined $5,500.
1985	John David Munday	Went over in a plastic barrel. He was arrested.
1989	Jeff Petrovic and Peter Dibernadi	Went over in a steel barrel. They were the first two-person team to go over and survive.
1990	Jessi Sharp	Went over in a polyethylene kayak. He was never found.
1995	Steve Trotter and Lori Martin	Went over in a metal cylinder and lived.
1995	Robert Overacker	Went over on a jet ski with a parachute attached. He died when his parachute failed.

In 1960, Roger Woodward, who was seven years old, went over the falls after a boating accident. He went over the falls with only his life jacket on and lived! He was picked up by the Maid of the Mist, and he had only a few facial bruises. He was a very lucky boy!

Activities

Make a time line of the daredevils who went over Niagara Falls.

Make a list of the dangers involved in going over Niagara Falls.

What do you think people would have considered when they were building barrels to go over the falls?

Check out Thunder Alley at *www.iaw.com* for more information.

The Moving Falls

How Erosion Has Changed Niagara Falls Over the Centuries

Look at the map on the next page. You will see that Niagara Falls used to be much further north on the Niagara River. What happened? How did the falls move so far up river?

The answer is erosion. The bottom of the river is rock, but underneath the rock is softer dirt. As the water pours over the edge of the rock, the force of the water washes away the dirt underneath. As more dirt washes away, the rocks crash down into the river bottom, and the falls move back. Then the process starts all over again.

Erosion can happen anywhere. If soil is not protected by plants and trees, then the rain can wash the top of the soil right away. This is a big problem for farmers. The good soil can wash away if the land is not planted correctly. The Grand Canyon in the United States was formed by a little river that eroded away the land over millions of years.

Wind can also cause erosion by blowing dry soil away. This also helped to form the Grand Canyon. Deserts suffer much erosion because there is nothing to hold down the dirt when the wind blows.

Niagara Falls used to be at the end of Niagara River where it empties into Lake Ontario. Over the last 12,300 years, the falls have moved 7.1 miles or 11.4 kilometers down the river to where they are today. The geologists estimate that in about 8,000 years, Niagara Falls might move all the way to Lake Erie!

Look at the map on the following page and answer these questions about erosion.

1. If Niagara Falls has moved 11.4 kilometers (7 miles) in 12,300 years, what is its average change per year? _____

2. What would be some things that would affect the rate of erosion? _____

   _____

3. How far did the falls erode in the last 2,000 years? _____

4. How far did they erode from 700 years ago until 1795? _____

5. How long did it take for the falls to move from the edge of Lake Ontario to where the Rainbow Bridge is today? _____

6. How long ago did the falls split into two separate falls? _____

Hint: Fold this section under before reproducing.

Answers: 1. .93 meters/1.017 yards **2.** wind, soil and rock types, glaciers **3.** 7.5 k/4.66 miles **4.** 2.67 k/1.66 miles **5.** 10,000 years **6.** 700 years ago

The Moving Falls *(cont.)*

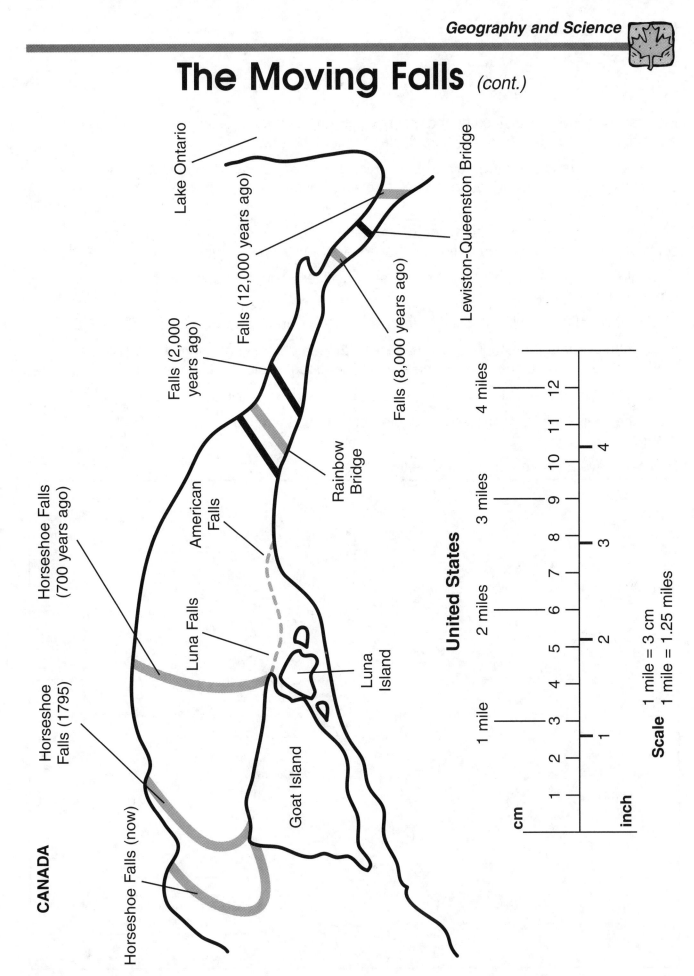

Lake Ontario

Falls (12,000 years ago)

Lewiston-Queenston Bridge

Falls (2,000 years ago)

Falls (8,000 years ago)

Rainbow Bridge

Horseshoe Falls (700 years ago)

American Falls

Horseshoe Falls (1795)

Luna Falls

Luna Island

Horseshoe Falls (now)

Goat Island

CANADA

United States

1 mile | 2 miles | 3 miles | 4 miles

cm

inch

Scale 1 mile = 3 cm
1 mile = 1.25 miles

Riding the Metro

Montreal has a very clean, safe, and modern subway system. It is easy and cheap to get around the city on the subway. The subway is called the Metro.

Montreal is a French-speaking city. Many of the subway stations have French names. The subway stations are decorated in many interesting ways. Some people like to ride the subway just to visit the stations!

The subway has four lines. Each line uses a different color. You can follow one color to get somewhere. Sometimes you need to change colors to reach your destination.

Look at the map below. You can color the subway lines. You will need four colors: orange, green, blue, and yellow.

Find St. Michel, then follow the line to the left until you find Snowdon. Color that line blue.

Find Honore-Beaugrand, then follow that line to the left until you go through Berri-Uqam, McGill, Atwater, and Lionel Groulx and end at Angrignon. Color that line green.

Find Berri-Uqam, then follow that line until you come to Longueuil. Color that line yellow.

Color the remaining horseshoe-shaped line from Henri-Bourassa around to Cote-Vertu with orange.

Now you have a colored map of the Metro.

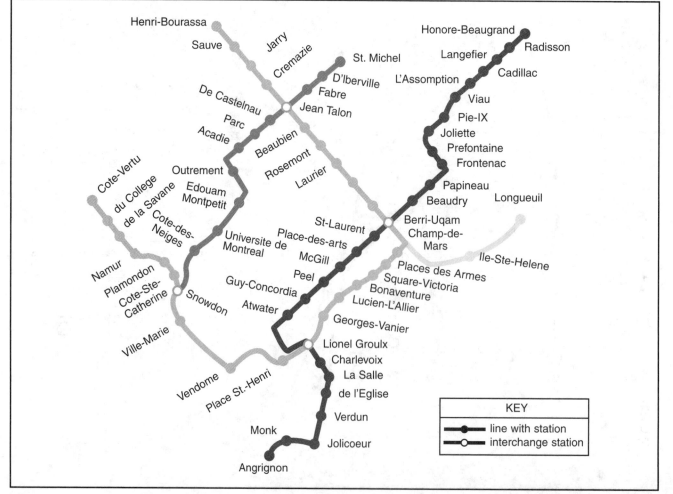

Riding the Metro *(cont.)*

Use your Metro map to answer these questions.

1. Name the four stations where you can change from one color line to another.

    _____   _____

    _____   _____

2. Which line is the shortest one? _____

3. How many stops are there on the orange line? _____

4. How many stations are there where the Green line crosses the Orange line? _____

5. Name the stations at the beginning and end of the Blue line. _____

6. Which line has the largest number of stops? _____

7. Which is the only line that crosses the river? _____

8. Use a black crayon or marker and trace the route you would take to go from Cadillac to Beaudry. Would you have to change lines? _____

9. Use a red crayon or marker and trace the route you would take to go from Verdun to Jarry. Would you have to change lines? _____

10. Show someone in your class how to get from Ville-Marie to Longueuil. Trace that route in another color.

Bonus Activities

*   Choose three of the stations and try to find out how they got their names. Some of the stations are named for famous places in France. Others are named for famous people.

*   Have you ever ridden on a subway? Write a story about what it was like. If you have never ridden a subway, write a story about what you think it would be like.

Hint: Fold this section under before reproducing.

Answers: 1. Snowden, Jean Talon, Berri-Uqam, Lionel Groulx **2.** yellow **3.** 28 **4.** 2
5. St. Michel and Snowden **6.** orange **7.** yellow **8.** no **9.** yes

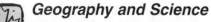

Measuring the Temperature

In the United States, the Fahrenheit scale is used to measure temperature. In the Fahrenheit scale, water freezes at 32 degrees, and water boils at 210 degrees at sea level.

In Canada and most other countries of the world, the Celsius scale is used. In the Celsius (or centigrade) scale, water freezes at 0 degrees and boils at 100 degrees at sea level.

Here is a chart that compares some Fahrenheit and Celsius temperatures.

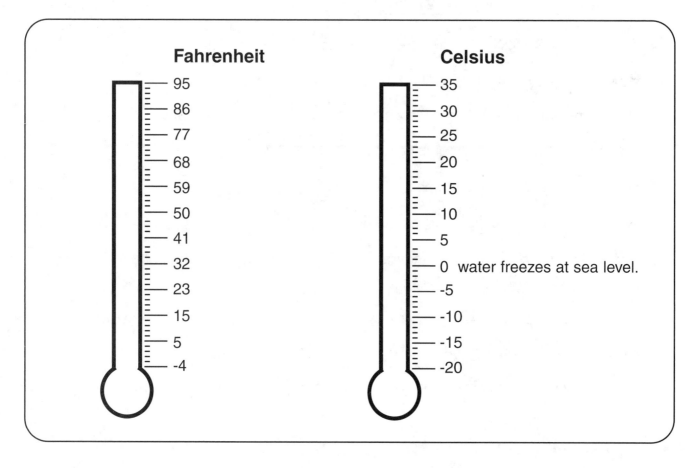

You can see that temperatures look lower using the Celsius scale. On the Fahrenheit scale, 35 degrees would be very cold outside, but on the Celsius scale, it is very hot!

If the temperature changes by 10 degrees on the centigrade scale, it changes by 18 degrees on the Fahrenheit scale.

How Cold Is It?

Use the temperature chart on the last page to decide what temperature would be good for these activities. Compare your answers with other students in your class. Why would some people have different answers?

swimming outside

_____ °F

_____ °C

snowmobiling

_____ °F

_____ °C

ice skating outside

_____ °F

_____ °C

hiking

_____ °F

_____ °C

playing softball

_____ °F

_____ °C

playing ice hockey outside

_____ °F

_____ °C

having a picnic

_____ °F

_____ °C

water skiing

_____ °F

_____ °C

boating

_____ °F

_____ °C

making a snowman

_____ °F

_____ °C

Lobster—A Creature of the Sea

In the Maritime provinces of Nova Scotia, New Brunswick, and Prince Edward Island, many of the people earn their living from the sea. One of the animals from the sea is the lobster. The lobster that comes from that part of the world is best.

Lobsters are animals that live in the ocean. They live on the ocean floor in burrows or holes. They watch and wait for small fish, crabs, snails, or other lobsters to come along. The lobster will grab its prey with its front claws. At night lobsters walk around on the floor of the ocean looking for food.

Lobsters do not have backbones. They are called crustaceans, which means "hard shell." Their hard shell protects them.

Many people like to eat lobster. Lobsters are usually dark green or dark blue, but their shells turn red when they are cooked. Lobsters are caught in traps that are called "lobster pots." Fishermen set the traps on the floor of the ocean then go back later and pull them up. If they are lucky, they will find a lobster in the trap.

On the next page, there is a picture of a lobster. Can you read the clues and decide how to label each part of the lobster?

The **eye** is small, round, and black.

The **claw** is big and is used to catch other animals.

The **brain** is very small and is close to the front.

The **stomach** has a tube, which is the mouth of the lobster.

The **liver** looks like the largest organ in the body.

The **heart** is just above the liver.

The **intestine** runs through the tail of the lobster.

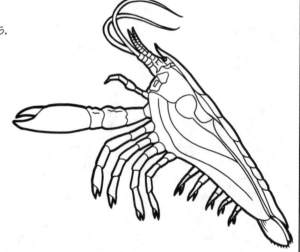

Color the lobster picture and hang it up for everyone to see.

- -

Hint: Fold this section under before reproducing.

Answers for page 35: 1. claw **2.** eye **3.** brain **4.** stomach **5.** stomach **6.** liver **7.** intestine

34

Lobster—A Creature of the Sea (cont.)

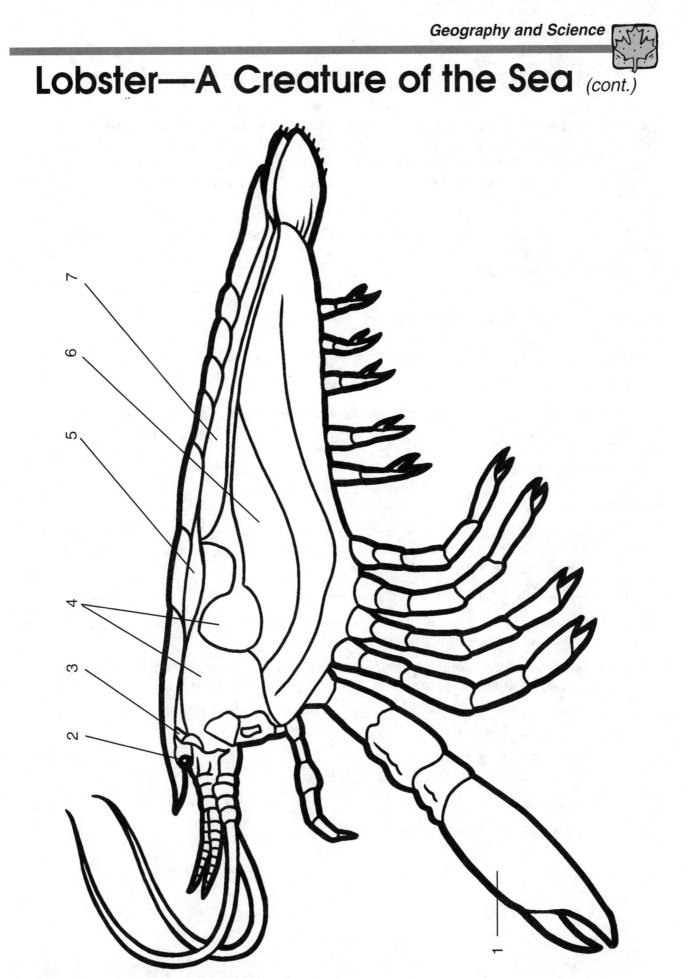

Nature's Wonderful Light Show

The *aurora borealis* is a magnificent display of colors that is found when electricity charged particles called electrons and protons rush into the earth at the top and bottom of the globe. They are attracted there because of a magnetic field around the poles. When the sun erupts in solar flares, many more electrons and protons rush in and the displays of the dancing lights are formed.

The aurora borealis can appear as large curtains of shimmering colored lights that hang from the sky. Purple, blue, green, pink, yellow, and orange are colors that appear in the sky. At times these "northern lights" can cover the entire sky.

Creating Your Own Aurora Borealis

Materials

- watercolor paper (or the heaviest white paper available)
- water colors–blue, black, purple, red, yellow, orange, green, dark blue-black
- rubber cement
- brushes

Directions

1. Find pictures of the aurora borealis. There are many lovely pictures on the Internet and in books. *Arctic Son* has pictures of the aurora. Science books about weather and magnetism often have pictures of the aurora.

2. Think and talk about the colors that you see.

3. Use a toothpick to put a few small dots of rubber cement on the white paper. This will be where stars would be. Let the rubber cement dry.

4. Using light colors with plenty of water, color going down the page in a vertical direction on the paper. Use enough water to let the colors flow. Let the colors dry.

5. Using the dark blue-black paint silhouettes of a tree, an old cabin, an arctic animal or other interesting things on the foreground of the painting.

6. Next use more of your dark paint and a little more water. Cover the rubber cement and paint around the sky and land. The aurora borealis is best seen at night.

7. Let the paper dry.

8. Remove the rubber cement and look at your aurora borealis.

Let's Write Some Poetry!

Pretty things like the northern lights often inspire us to write poetry. Let's see what we can write about the aurora borealis.

Cinquain

Cinquains are poems that are fun and easy to write. They are called cinquains because they have five lines. Follow this pattern to write a cinquain about the beautiful northern lights.

1. On your first line, write one word for a title.

2. On your second line, write two words that describe your first word.

3. On your third line, write an action word and two other words about the first line.

4. On your fourth line, write four words that express feelings about the title word.

5. On your fifth line, write a synonym for your first word.

Example

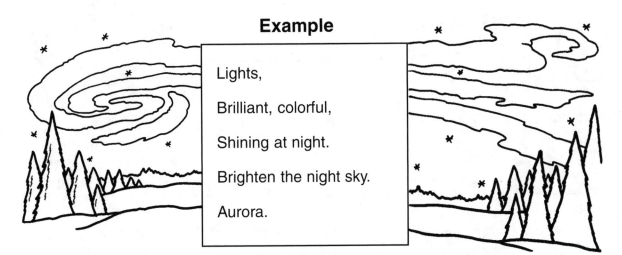

Lights,

Brilliant, colorful,

Shining at night.

Brighten the night sky.

Aurora.

Write your cinquain on the lines below. Try writing cinquains about other topics that you have studied.

_____

_____ _____

_____ _____ _____

_____ _____ _____ _____

_____

Haiku Poetry

Haiku are Japanese poems that are very short. These poems are only three lines. You have to count the syllables in the lines. The poem should have a total of 17 syllables.

1. The first and third lines each contain five syllables.
2. The second line contains seven syllables.

Haiku should be short snapshots of something that you see around you.

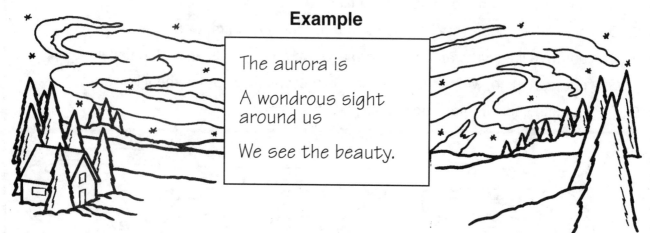

Example

The aurora is

A wondrous sight
around us

We see the beauty.

Remember that these poems do not have to rhyme.

Write your haiku on the lines below.

_____

_____

_____

What other things in nature can you write a haiku about?

Share your poetry with your classmates.

Suggested Reading: *Arctic Son* by Jean Craighead George (See bibliography for more information.)

History of Canada

Important Events in Canadian History

30,000 B.C.	People entered the Arctic via the Bering Strait.
3,000 B.C.	The Inuit people arrive.
1,000 A.D.	The first North American settlement is established by Leif Eriksson at L'anse aux Meadows in Newfoundland.
1497	John Cabot explores Newfoundland and Labrador and claims land for England.
1534–1535	Jacques Cartier explores the Gulf of St. Lawrence and claims Acadia for France.
1605	Pierre de Monts founds the first successful colony at Port Royal Nova Scotia.
1608	Samuel de Champlain founds Quebec City.
1670	Hudson Bay Company formed and created a trading network in eastern and central Canada.
1713	Treaty of Utrecht gave much of eastern Canada to Great Britain from France.
1756–1763	The Seven Years War between France and Great Britain. This is called the French and Indian War in the United States. The Acadians are expelled from Nova Scotia, New Brunswick, and Prince Edward Island. France gives up its colonies in Canada.
1774	The Quebec Act grants French Canadians political and religious rights.
1783	The Loyalists arrive in New Brunswick.
1785	St. John, New Brunswick, is the first official city in Canada.
1789	Alexander Mackenzie canoes down the Mackenzie River. He thought he had found the water route to the Pacific, but the river led to the Arctic Ocean.
1812–1815	The British fight the United States in many battles along the Canadian border.

1867	Canada buys the Northwest Territory from the Hudson Bay Company.
1870	The Red River Rebellion
1873	The Royal Canadian Mounted Police are founded and originally called the North West Mounted Police.
1884	Native potlatch ceremony and ceremonial dances are banned in British Columbia.
1885	The Canadian Pacific Railroad is finished coast to coast; second Metis rebellion.
1896	Gold is discovered in the Yukon.
1914–1918	Canadian troops fight for Britain in World War I.
1918	Women get the right to vote.
1931	Canadian independence from Great Britain is granted by the Statute of Westminster.
1939–1945	Canadians fight in World War II in Europe and the Pacific.
1943	The Alaska Highway is completed.
1950	The Inuit people get the right to vote in federal elections.
1959	The Saint Lawrence Seaway is completed.
1967	Montreal hosted the Expo 67 World s Fair
1976	Montreal host the Summer Olympics
1986	Vancouver hosted the Expo 86 World s Fair
1988	Calgary hosts the Winter Olympics.
1993–1994	The Toronto Bluejays win the World Series two years in a row.
1994	Cod fishing is banned due to declining fish populations.
1998	The second referendum for Quebec to become independent is narrowly defeated.
1999	The Nunavit Territory is formed.

40

Making a Time Line

Time lines are used to show when things happened in history. A time line shows the order of events in chronological order. Chronological means in the order that they happened. Use the steps on this page to make a time line of your own life.

1. List ten important things that have happened to you in your life. Remember to put the date that the event happened. If you do not remember the exact day, try to remember the month and year.

2. Number the events in the order that they happened. Put a number one next to the first thing that happened, a two by the next thing, and so on until all the events are numbered. This is how you put things into chronological order.

3. Put the six most important events on the time line below. Remember to keep them in chronological order.

My Life Time Line

By _____

_____

Bonus Activity: Make a time line using 10 of the events in the list of important dates in Canadian history. What dates did you choose? Why?

Time Line Game

On the following pages is a Canadian history time line game. Explain to your students what a time line is and have them complete their personal time lines. After they have finished their time lines, have them discuss why they chose the events that they did for their time line. Have them display their time lines. They might want to make larger ones on long sheets of paper.

Explain to the class that the Time Line Game is also a time line, even though it is not straight. It presents key events in the history of Canada.

The game is a simple board game. Use buttons or beans for markers. Copy the four pages of the game and tape them together to make a game board for each group of 4–6 players. Make a spinner to go with each game board. You may want students to color their game boards and then laminate them for future use.

Each student spins the spinner. The one with the highest number starts, then go clockwise around the group. The students take turns spinning, moving, and following the directions on the board. The first student to the end wins. To make the end more challenging, you may require that the winner has the exact number he or she needs to reach the last space.

The purpose of the game is for students to learn some of the major events in Canadian history. Each student should be given a chance to finish the game even after the first player reaches the end.

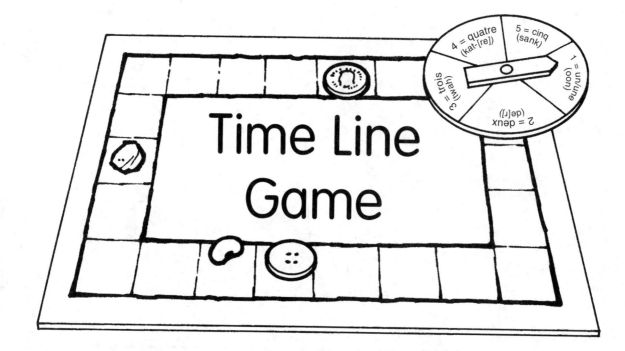

Time Line Game *(cont.)*

D

1950 AD

Inuit people get the right to vote in federal elections.

1959 AD

The St. Lawrence Seaway opens.

1988 AD

Calgary hosts the Winter Olympics.

Name your favorite winter sport.

Directions

- Cut this time line section along the dashed lines.

- Attach it to another game section by matching the tabs.

- Glue the four sections to a large piece of construction paper.

1994 AD

Cod fishing is banned.

Go back 2 spaces.

1998 AD

The second referendum for Quebec's independence is narrowly defeated.

1999 AD

Nunavut is the newest territory!

You Win!

A

Time Line Game *(cont.)*

1896 AD

Gold discovered in the Yukon.

Cheer Loudly!

1885 AD

The Canadian Pacific Railroad is completed coast to coast.

Walk around your chair.

1873 AD

Northwest Canadian Mounties are formed.

Name someone dressed in red clothes.

C

1918 AD

Canadian women get the right to vote.

Cheer loudly and move ahead 1 space.

1931 AD

Statute of Westminster grants Canada independence from England.

1939–45 AD

Canada joins the Allies in WWII

D

Directions

• Cut this time line section along the dashed lines.

• Attach it to another game section by matching the tabs.

• Glue the four sections to a large piece of construction paper.

Time Line Game *(cont.)*

1870 AD

The Red River Rebellion

Go back 1 space.

C

1867 AD

Canada buys the Northwest territory from the Hudson Bay Company.

1789 AD

Alexander Mackenzie canoes down the Mackenzie River.

Name another explorer.

1774 AD

The Quebec Act grants French Canadians religious and political rights.

Move ahead 2 spaces.

1756–63 AD

Seven Years War—the Acadians are expelled from the Maritime area.

Go back 4 spaces.

1713 AD

Treaty of Utrecht grants much of France's lands to Great Britain.

Directions

- Cut this time line section along the dashed lines.

- Attach it to another game section by matching the tabs.

- Glue the four sections to a large piece of construction paper.

B

Time Line Game (cont.)

B

1670 AD

Hudson Bay Company formed.

Move ahead 1 space

1608 AD

Samuel de Champlain founds Quebec City.

Pat yourself on the back.

1534 AD

Jacques Cartier claims Acadia for France

Directions

- Cut this time line section along the dashed lines.

- Attach it to another game section by matching the tabs.

- Glue the four sections to a large piece of construction paper.

10,000 BC–5,000 BC
You start here!

A

1,000 AD

Leif Ericksson establishes the first European settlement in North America.

Move ahead 2 spaces.

1497 AD

John Cabot claims Newfoundland for England.

Stand and cheer!

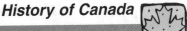

Time Line Game (cont.)

Copy the spinner circle and arrow below and glue to lightweight cardboard. Cut out the circle and the arrow. Punch a hole in the center of the circle and at the indicated spot on the arrow. Color the spinner with bright colors but let the numbers show. Attach the arrow to the spinner with a brass paper fastener.

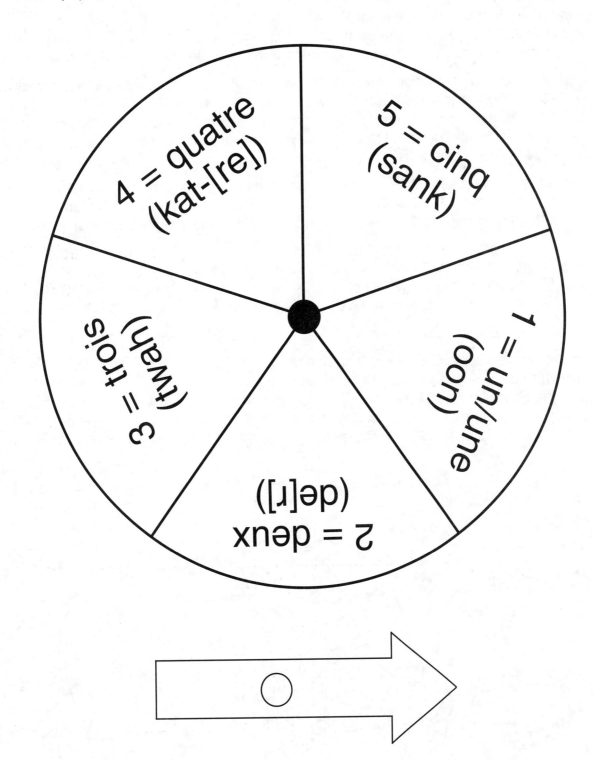

Dinosaurs Roamed the West

More dinosaur remains have been found in the Alberta Badlands than anywhere else on Earth. Alberta has so many remains there, that they have a park named Dinosaur Provincial Park near Brooks, Alberta. There have been over 35 species of dinosaurs found in this area.

The Alberta Badlands is very dry and rocky. It is hard to believe that millions of years ago the ocean was there. The Western Interior Seaway covered much of what is now Alberta, Saskatchewan, and Manitoba. The climate was mild and densely forested with great sequoia-like trees. Large sea creatures lived in the water, and great dinosaurs roamed the earth.

The Albertosaurus was a relative of the Tyrannosaurus; it had a huge head, jagged teeth, and sharp claws on bird-like feet. Albertosarus was about six meters (6.5 yards) tall and ten meters (11 yards) long and was one of the largest carnivores to have ever lived on land. It had dagger-like teeth and powerful jaws. Like Tyrannosaurus, it possessed tiny forearms and large and well-muscled hind legs.

The Edmontosaurus walked on four legs and ate vegetation; it probably lived in herds. Edmontosaurus, or "Edmonton lizard" takes its name from the Edmonton rock formation. It was one of the largest and last of the duckbilled dinosaurs and weighed 2.7 metric tons (three tons).

The Edmontonia was about 7 meters (23 feet) long and had hard, bony-plated armor covering. Huge spikes stuck out of its shoulders. It has a wedge-shaped head. It grew to a length of five meters (16 feet) and weighed almost three tons.

Notice that these dinosaurs were named for the area where they were found.

Another important dinosaur discovery was named for Lawrence Lambe. He was a very important Canadian paleontologist. The Lambeosaurus (which means "Lambe's lizard") is on display at the Royal Ontario Museum in Toronto, Ontario. The Lambeosaurus was about 15 meters (49 feet) long and had a large, hollow crest on its head. Scientists believe that the hollow crest allowed the dinosaur to make loud honks and bellows that echoed across the land.

Many other types of dinosaurs have been discovered in this area, and tourists visit the Royal Tyrrell Museum of Palaeontology in Drumheller, Alberta, to see the variety of dinosaurs discovered.

Dinosaur Jumble—A Paleontological Challenge

When archeologists look for dinosaur remains and other artifacts from the past, they go to a "dig." A dig is a place where the conditions are right for finding remains. In Alberta there are many digs.

Paleontologists do not just go somewhere and start digging. They have a plan and a particular way of looking for things. They decide where a good place to search is. Then they mark off that area in a grid. A grid divides an area into small squares. Each square of the grid has a letter and a number. When paleontologists find something in a particular square, they can accurately record where they were and what they found there. Then when the excavation is finished, all of the pieces from the squares can be put together like a giant jigsaw puzzle.

You can take your class on a mini-paleontological dig.

Materials

- a large, shallow, plastic bin or cardboard box (like an under-the-bed storage box)
- enough sand to fill the box
- dinosaur pieces (Laminate and cut up the dinosaur pictures on pages 51–53.)
- string
- tape
- some old paint brushes of various sizes (be sure to include some very small ones)
- a piece of paper
- a pencil or pen
- a bucket or another box

Directions

1. Fill the box with sand. Put the dinosaur pieces into the sand. Be sure to mix up the pieces and scatter them around.

2. Use the string to make a grid across the top of the box. Tape two pieces going lengthwise and three going across. Make sure you space the string evenly so the box is divided into 12 small squares.

3. Have the students draw matching grids on their papers. Label the horizontal rows with letters and the vertical columns with numbers. Your squares will be A1, A2, A3, A4, B1, etc.

4. Instruct the students to carefully brush away the sand in one square until they find something. Tell them to record on another paper what they found and where they found it. Put the sand that they take away into a bucket or other container.

5. After the students find all of the dinosaur pieces, have them reassemble the dinosaurs and display them in the room.

Dinosaur Jumble—A Paleontological Challenge *(cont.)*

Extension Activities

- Encourage the children to take their time and work carefully. Discuss how the age of a find can be determined by how deeply it is buried. Try burying one of the dinosaurs deeper than the others to reinforce this idea.

- Try burying one of the dinosaurs relatively "intact" so that the students can see how a grid will help them get the whole picture when they are done.

- Discuss why some dinosaur remains would be found intact, while others might be found jumbled up or incomplete. Bury one of the dinosaurs with some pieces missing. What problems would that cause for archeologists? How would they go about figuring out what the missing pieces were like?

- Talk to the students about what they find on an actual dig. They will be finding pieces of dinosaurs but on a dig they would only find bones.

- Discuss with them how bones become fossils when they are buried for a long time.

- Try burying other things in the sand. Would human artifacts be buried deeper or shallower? Put in things like plastic bottle caps, paper clips, etc. Talk to the children about why these things would not be buried as deeply as the dinosaur bones.

- Discuss how the things we use today might become treasures to archeologists of the future.

- Have your class do a time capsule. Put in things that are important to them. Have them write about what people will think of their items in 25 years, 50 years, 100 years.

Dinosaur Jumble—A Paleontological Challenge *(cont.)*

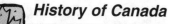

Dinosaur Jumble—An
Paleontological Challenge *(cont.)*

52

Dinosaur Jumble—A
Paleontological Challenge *(cont.)*

Aaron's Archeological Adventure

Aaron had always liked walking through the woods home. He knew that Native Americans had walked there and had also gone down to the creek because he had found a few points and pottery scattered nearby. He often thought to himself, "I would rather have been a Native American boy who was learning to shoot his bow, ride his pony, or play the ball games with the other boys of the tribe than go to school and sit at a desk."

On good weather days, it was even harder to make himself concentrate on his reading assignment. But today the teacher said something that caught his attention. "Boys and girls," she said, "I would like to read to you a story about the Native American tribe called the Kwakiutl that lived in this territory before many of your family came to British Columbia."

Aaron turned his full attention to his teacher. He listened carefully as she talked about the way the Kwakiutl had made their homes near creeks and how they had hunted and fished in the area. When the teacher finished reading. Aaron raised his hand to add that they had seen such a tribe near the creek by his home. The other children chuckled for Aaron always had a good imagination. Once when he broke out a window at his grandparent's house, he told them that the Native Americans did it. Aaron didn't care. He knew that the Haida had lived near his home, and he would prove it. Suddenly, Aaron realized that the time had passed quickly and the school bus was there, waiting to pick up the children. Aaron boarded the bus with his little sister Christa and his younger brother Jared.

As Aaron had boarded bus 14, Joe the driver asked if he had found any new sites this week. Aaron liked pretending that he was an archeologist and he was always digging somewhere to uncover a great civilization

"Yes," he responded. "I think I have found a very old site, but I will need help to dig before the ground freezes. I will need some very strong and courageous explorers."

"I'll help," said Christa eagerly.

"Me, too!" added Jared. He was the youngest and did not like to be left out of things.

"You aren't afraid of the wolves and bears?" Aaron asked.

"Nope," they replied bravely. "We'll just take good old Jake with us."

Jake was their fearless Welsh Corgi. He loved to go exploring as much as the kids did. After all, he was a descendant of the Queen's corgis.

Aaron's Archeological Adventure *(cont.)*

As soon as the bus stopped, the three children nearly flew to the house. "Mom, can you make our snack to go? We have an important dig to do down by the creek and we're in a real hurry!"

Their mother smiled as she packed some sandwiches and juice and waved good-bye to the fearless explorers. She was used to their great adventures.

Their wagon became a pack horse to carry their supplies. They needed lots of shovels, brushes, hats, an extra canteen, mosquito repellent, string, drawing paper, and pencils for writing important notes.

It was a challenge to get all of the supplies in the wagon, but they needed everything.

When they reached the creek, Aaron began giving orders, but his brother and sister ignored him. Jared decided to eat his snack first. Christa went off to draw the butterflies that were dancing around the plants by the stream.

"Well, I'll just have to map out our plan without you two," Aaron said as he stomped off.

Something told him to move up above the ledge where a partial opening had been formed in the rock below. This will be a good place. He began staking out the ground and used his string to divide the small area into a grid. He carefully copied the grid on a piece of paper, then he chose a section of the ground to begin his dig. He worked very carefully to remove the dirt, and he checked each piece carefully for any signs of gold or relics.

He was getting rather hot, so he grabbed his hat from the wagon and proceeded to dig some more. He heard a clunk and another, so he stopped and removed several large, round stones and put them to the side hoping to find a piece of flint or another point.

By this time, his partners had finished their snacks and had come to help. But a snarling gray wolf stood between them and Aaron's dig. The wolf had been awakened by all the noise in his den and he was not happy. Christa and Jared stopped still in their tracks. Jake hid behind them.

Aaron thought fast. He leaned down like Goliath and picked up a stone and gave it a toss at the wolf to divert his attention toward him. When the wolf looked away, Christa and Jared scurried up the nearest tree, and now Jake was growling and standing his ground. Dad heard all of the commotion and came running with his old 22. He saw the terror in the eyes of Aaron and he saw the wolf. He fired. Dad was a good shot, so he knew that he could make the wolf take flight if the bullet just skidded past him. The wolf took off quickly.

Aaron's Archeological
Adventure *(cont.)*

Jared and Christa came down the tree to hug Dad, and Jake jumped up on everyone. Aaron came down from the ledge. Dad picked up the round stone that Aaron had hurled to sidetrack the wolf. He examined it carefully. "Looks like you've had an exciting day, Aaron. You've found a boiling stone and there must be others." Aaron looked at the interesting stones. He was proud of his archeological find.

With Dad's help the children dug up other stones, and sure enough, the nicely rounded stones had zigzag cracks from being repeatedly heated by fire and plunged into water.

"It's a good thing some family set up camp here many moons ago. They never knew they helped save you from a wolf!" They all laughed and headed home to tell Mom about their exciting adventure.

The next day in class, Mrs. Barhorst called on Aaron to share why he had brought so many round stones to school. The other children thought, "What whopper of a story will Aaron tell today."

And he did.

What Are Boiling Stones?

These large, smooth, round stones were chosen by the women to help in the preparation of food. The stones were heated in their fire until red hot. Then they were taken out of the fire and dipped into water to get rid of the ashes. Next, the hot stones were put in a basket or box that could hold water. Then another basket full of food was placed into the water. This worked like a modern-day steamer to keep the food hot. More hot stones could be added to the basket or the box as needed until the cooking was finished.

The waterproof boxes were made from a single piece of wood and sewn together by using spruce root.

Flat stones were also collected and heated. They would be cleaned and placed in a pit and food would be placed on top to bake.

56

Aaron's Archeological Adventure *(cont.)*

Activities

- Bring in some different size and shape of stones and let the class decide which ones would be good for cooking or baking.

- Put different sizes and colors of stones in the sunlight and see which ones warm up fastest. How long do the stones hold the heat?

- Have students notice how brick buildings will warm up in the sun and remain warm for a long time. Are the boiling stones like anything that is used today?

- Refer to the Dinosaur Jumble activity for further activities with palentology.

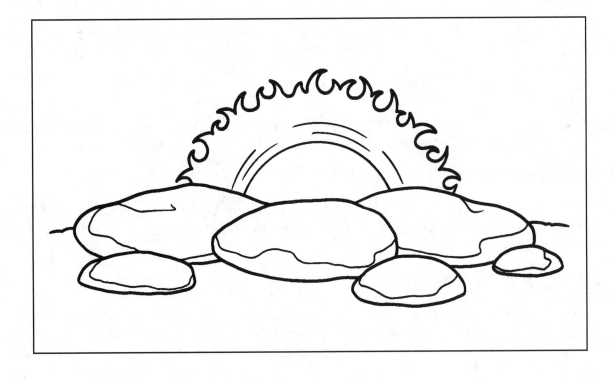

Making Fossils

One important clue that archeologists use to study the past is fossils. Fossils are imprints of bones, plants, animals, and other things that are trapped in the soil. After millions of years, the soil turns to rock, and these imprints are trapped forever in the layers of the rocks.

Fossils are almost like an ancient form of photography, and archeologists can study these "pictures" of the ancient world to learn new things.

You can make your own fossils.

Materials

- small aluminum pans or baking dishes.

- You can also use paper or plastic bowls.

- Plaster of Paris

- Feathers, shells, leaves, small plants, or other interesting things you find lying around outside on the ground

Directions

1. Follow the directions for mixing the Plaster of Paris

2. Pour the Plaster of Paris into your bowl. Make your layer of plaster about an inch deep. Remember that the thinner you make your layer of plaster, the sooner it will dry.

3. Let the plaster dry until it is not wet but still soft.

4. Impress your shell, leaf, or whatever you are using into the very top of the plaster. Do not push down too hard but be sure to leave an imprint of your item. Do not leave the item in the plaster.

5. Let the plaster finish drying, and then remove it from the bowl.

6. Now you have a fossil of your item. You can use your project for a paperweight or a decoration. You can use paints to color your fossil if you like.

Cultural Areas Jigsaw Puzzle

The Native American tribes of Canada lived in six distinct areas. These regions shaped the cultures of the tribes through geography, climate, and resources. For instance, groups that lived in the north had to learn how to survive in very cold climates with few plants. The tribes of the eastern woodlands had trees and plants to help with their housing and food.

Northwest

These people lived along the coast of the Pacific. They relied largely on the ocean and rivers for fishing, especially salmon. The Northwest tribes developed a complex society, which emphasized art. Large totem poles decorated the villages and complex masks were used in many of their ceremonies. This area included the Kwakiutl, Haida, and Tlingit tribes.

Arctic

The Inuit people learned to survive in this very harsh climate. They were a hunting and fishing society that created many tools to help them. These people used dog sleds to help them travel throughout the arctic in search of food. Harpoons and bows and arrows helped them in their hunts, and igloos would protect them as they wandered across the cold, snow-covered tundra.

Subarctic Northern Hunters

The Ojibwa, Chipewyan, and Naskapi were tribes that hunted the northern areas of the subarctic. These people created snowshoes to help them travel across the winter landscape. They would hunt bear, caribou, rabbit, beaver, moose, and other animals of the north. Many of these tribes would travel the area following the herds or go south to Lake Huron to fish in the summer.

Eastern Woodlands

These people relied on hunting and farming for their food. Because they farmed, they had established villages that sometimes had as many as 2,000 inhabitants. The tribe of the Northeast included the powerful League of the Iroquois. This political and military force included five tribes, the Mohawk, Onondaga, Seneca, Oneida, and Cayuga. Other tribes of the Northeast area included Mi'kmaq, Huron, Erie, Algonquain, and Ottawa.

Plains

The people of the plains were great hunters. Their skill in hunting bison provided them with food, clothing, tools, and utensils. Before horses were introduced by the Spanish, the plains people hunted bison on foot, sometimes driving the buffalo over the edges of cliffs to kill them. The bow and arrow allowed hunting from a safe distance. The tepees of the plains tribes are a symbol of their nomadic way of life.

Plateau

The high plateau between the Rockies and the Cascade Mountains was home to 25 tribes. These people lived in partially underground homes in the winter, and in the summer they camped in teepee-like lodges. They mainly ate salmon and edible roots, but some traded with the Plains people for other items.

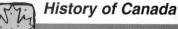

Cultural Areas Jigsaw Puzzle *(cont.)*

Use the map on the following page to make a jigsaw puzzle of the cultural areas of the native people of Canada. Copy the map on heavier paper and cut it into pieces along the heavy lines. Challenge a classmate to put the puzzle together.

Comparing and Contrasting

When you compare things, you look for things that are the same.

When you contrast things, you look for things that are different.

Think about the tribes on the map and fill in the following chart.

Compare and Contrast

	Assiniboine	Haida	Mi'kmaq	Inuit
Food				
Housing				
Method of Gathering Food				

Cultural Areas of Canada Map

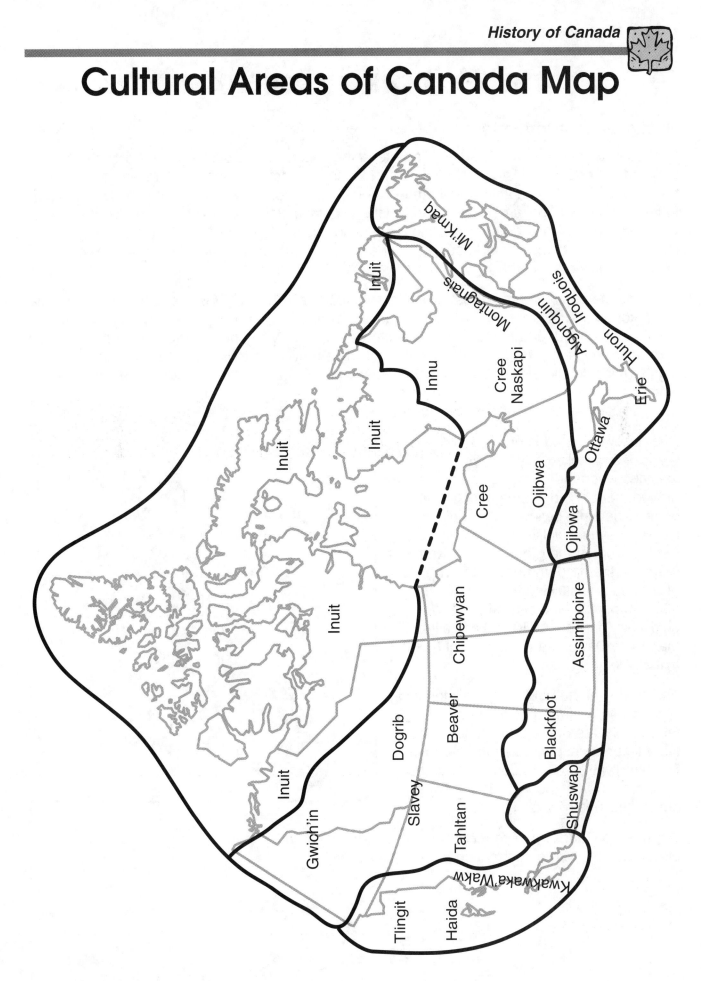

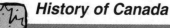
The Klondike Gold Rush

Background Information

In 1896 gold was discovered in the Klondike in the Yukon. The discovery started one of the largest gold rushes in history. The first man to discover the gold was Robert Henderson. He told about his find to another man named George Washington Carmack, but told Carmack not to let his friends Skookum Jim and Tagish Charley stake claims. His racist remarks enraged Carmack, who went over the hill and found a richer claim along another branch of the river. By the time Henderson heard about the richer fields, Carmack had told everyone else and all of the claims were staked.

This was the beginning of a great influx of gold seekers. Over 100,000 people started toward the Yukon to find their fortunes. Many hardships awaited these people as they faced harsh weather, little food, great mountains, and snow and mud. Many people died along the way. Sixty-four people died in an avalanche that hit while they were trying to cross Chilkoot Pass, a high formidable climb over the mountains. Many people gave up the quest as the conditions worsened on the journey. Those who made it to Dawson, the heart of the gold rush, found that conditions there were even worse.

Dawson was a muddy or snow-covered tent city that lacked any conveniences or services when the first gold rushers arrived there. Many of the people had been misled into believing that gold could be found by just walking around and picking it up off the ground. They were not ready for the hard and back-breaking work of digging and sluicing the gold. Of the 100,000 people who started out for the gold rush, only about 40,000 actually made it to Dawson and only about 5,000 actually found gold.

The stories of the gold rush are interesting to read and as varied as the people they tell about. One of the great American story tellers to experience the gold rush first hand was Jack London. His stories are told in *Call of the Wild*, *White Fang*, and collections of short stories.

Suggested Reading: *The Klondike Gold Rush* and *Gold! The Klondike Adventure.* (See bibliography for more information.)

Gold Fever!

During the Gold Rush the prospectors panned for gold. They did this by putting silt from the river or creek bottom into a shallow pan and gently shaking the pan until the dirt washed away, and the heavier gold nuggets and gold dust were left on the bottom of the pan. Then they would sort through the remaining rocks to find the gold nuggets.

Many gold camps had complicated systems of sluices. These were long, wooden troughs that were set on a downhill slope. Large amounts of dirt would be thrown into the sluice, then water would be released to run down the sluice and wash the dirt. The gold dust would be left behind in the crossbars of the sluice bottom. The principle was the same as panning, but much larger amounts of soil could be processed in less time.

Gold is a very valuable element. It never rusts, tarnishes, or corrodes. Things that are made of gold last forever and never lose their original look. Gold brings high prices. During the Klondike Gold Rush, an ounce of gold was worth 18 U.S. dollars that might not sound like much, but in today's money that would be about 800–900 U.S. dollars. An ounce of gold today sells for about 350–400 U.S. dollars. It is easy to see why people were willing to risk everything to go to the Klondike to search for gold.

Suggested Reading: *The Klondike Gold Rush* and *Gold! The Klondike Adventure.* (See bibliography for more information.)

Panning for "Gold"

Your students can practice panning for gold with this activity.

Materials

- sand
- small items to put in the sand
- mixed colors of beads of various sizes
- colanders
- small stones
- phony gold beads
- small wrapped candies

Directions

1. Mix the sand, small stones, and other items together. Make sure that the "prizes" are very few compared to the sand and stones.

2. The students will need to work over large pieces of paper or plastic.

3. Give each child or group of children a colander.

4. Put a large scoop of the sand mixture in each colander or have the students fill their colanders from a central workstation.

5. Give the children time to sift through the sand and find their prizes.

6. Discuss the following questions:

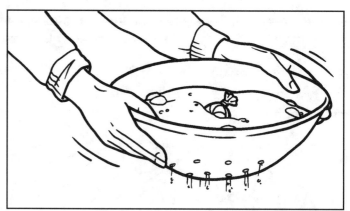

- What did you find in your pan?

- How did you feel about what you found? ·

- Who found the most "prizes"?

- Who found the fewest?

- Imagine that your whole future depended on what you found in your colander. How would you feel about what you found?

- Do you want to try again? Why or why not?

Yukon Gold Rush

Reference List for the Activity

Have the students think about the things that they would need to survive in the wilderness for one year. Have them think about how much they eat. What kinds of food would they need? Remember that there would be no prepared foods and that food would have to be prepared in some way. Also have the children think about how much the pack would weigh and how they would transport the items. The average weight for the supplies was 907 kg (2,000 pounds). How did people (on foot) get such large amounts of supplies around? The adventurers would divide up their packs and make several trips to get all of their supplies to the destinations.

Here is a suggested list of items to take to the Yukon. Have students discuss the need for each item.

- flour 68 kg (150 lbs.)
- bacon 68 kg (150 lbs.)
- beans 45 kg (100 lbs.)
- dried apples 11 kg (25 lbs.)
- dried peaches 11 kg (25 lbs.)
- dried apricots 11 kg (25 lbs.)
- rice 11 kg (25 lbs.)
- butter 11 kg (25 lbs.)
- granulated sugar 45 kg (100 lbs.)
- coffee 6.8 kg (15 lbs.)
- tea 8.6 kg (19 lbs.)
- salt 4.5 kg (10 lbs)
- pepper 0.45 kg (1 lb.)
- vinegar 3.8 L (1 gallon)
- 1 tent
- 1 frying pan
- 1 coffee pot
- 11 bars of soap
- 1 tine of matches
- 1 box of candles
- 1 medicine chest
- 1 pick
- 1 shovel
- 1 ax
- 1 gold pan
- 1 handsaw
- 1 hatchet
- 6 towels
- 1 sheet-iron stove
- nails 7.25 kg (16 lbs.)

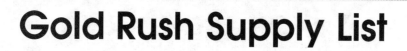

Gold Rush Supply List

Many people wanted to go look for gold in the Yukon. Some people did not know how long and hard the trip would be. In 1897 the government of Canada made the people take along enough supplies to last for one year.

These people had to cook, take care of themselves and their clothes, live in the wild, and protect themselves. What do you think it would take for you to survive for one year in the wilds of the Yukon?

On the lines below, make a list of the things that you would need to have to take on the gold rush. You might want to brainstorm with other classmates to make your list.

Item	Quantity
tent	1

66

Birchbark Canoes

Native peoples of North America developed the birchbark canoe to use as their main form of transportation. Since Canada has many rivers and lakes, people would use the water to get from one place to another. Using canoes made it easy to move people and things from one place to another.

Birchbark canoes were perfect for the people who lived in much of Canada. The birch tree grows over most of the area. Birchbark is light, smooth, tough and waterproof. It was easy to make the bark fit over the wooden frames. Birchbark canoes were light and easy to carry when they were empty.

Some birchbark canoes were small and carried only one or two people on hunting trips or other short journeys. Some of the canoes were used on lakes and rivers and were large enough for five people. Near the ocean, some people made ocean canoes that were 7 meters (22 feet) long and could carry six, eight, or ten people.

When the explorers came to North America, they found the canoe to be very useful. The French traders adopted the canoe and used it to help them on their hunting trips as they gathered furs and carried supplies.

The word "canoe" actually comes from the Caribbean natives who used dugout canoes called "kenu." The word was carried to the North by the French and Spanish explorers.

Have you ever been in a canoe? If you have, tell about your experiences. If you have not, find someone who has ridden in a canoe and ask him or her what it was like.

What makes a canoe move? The people in the canoe have paddles that they use to push against the water and propel the boat forward. When several people are paddling a canoe, it can move very quickly through the water.

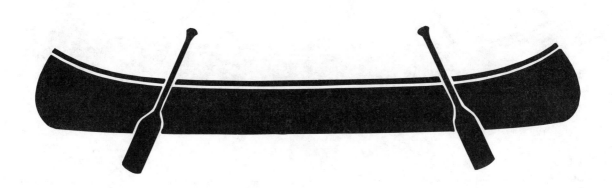

Make a Birchbark Canoe

On the next page is a pattern for a birchbark canoe. You can make your own canoe and display it in your classroom.

Materials

- canoe pattern on the next page
- scissors
  inch)

- tape
- *optional:* hole punch, yarn, 6.35 cm (2 1/2

  sticks or pipe cleaners (3–4)

Directions

1. Cut out the pattern on the next page. Make sure that you cut out on the thick black lines.

2. Cut the short, curved lines near the middle. These sections should be attached and are called the "bow" and the "stern."

3. Fold the canoe in the middle of the bottom along the dotted lines. Tape the ends of the canoe together.

4. Fold the bow and the stern up over the ends of the canoe. Tape them to the body of the canoe. These should help the canoe stay open on the top.

Optional: Use a hole punch to make holes where the ends of the canoe join and lace string or yarn through the holes to hold the boat together.

Put short sticks or pipe cleaners across the top of the canoe to look like a wooden frame.

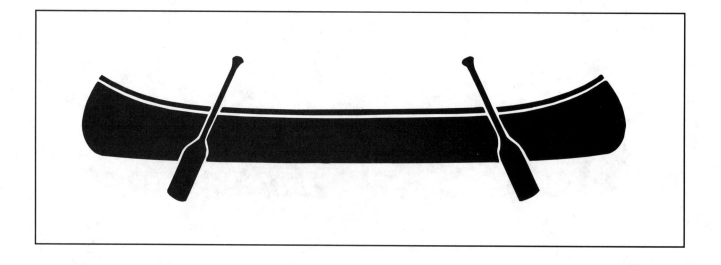

Make a Birchbark Canoe *(cont.)*

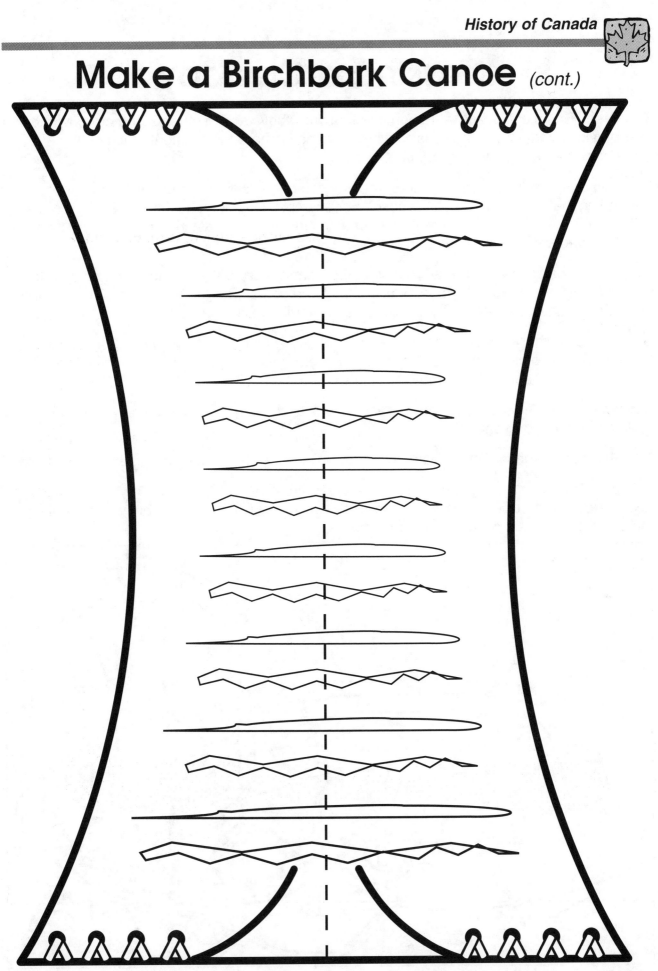

Dressing a Cowboy

The Great Plains of Canada were home to many cowboys and ranchers. The cowboy tradition is strong in Alberta. The traditional cowboy clothing is shared throughout much of the Americas, even as far away as South America.

Cowboys traveled light. They had to carry everything they owned with them on their horses. Everything that they wore had a purpose. For example, why do you think cowboys wore hats with wide brims? Remember, they did not have sunglasses. That's right! They wore hats with wide brims to keep the sun out of their eyes.

Many of the traditions of cowboy clothing came from the Spanish and Mexican riders. For instance, they were the ones to introduce chaps and spurs. But the traditions of these riders far to the south were adopted by cowboys as far north as Canada.

Sometimes cowboys who earned a little extra money would buy fancy boots or silver buckles for their belts. Some of the spurs worn by cowboys were very decorative and their boots sometimes cost as much as a two-week salary.

Cowboys today still wear much of the same practical clothing, although some things have been changed and updated.

Now think of reasons for other clothes the cowboys wore. Try to think about all of the different jobs a cowboy had to do.

Look at the picture of the cowboy on page 71. Color the picture and explain why each thing the cowboy wore was important to him.

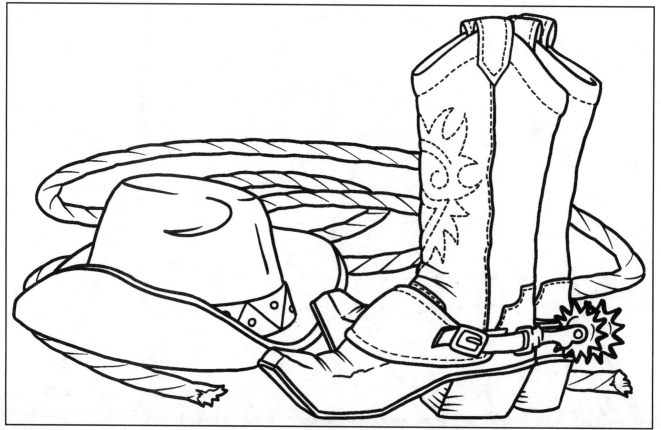

Dressing a Cowboy *(cont.)*

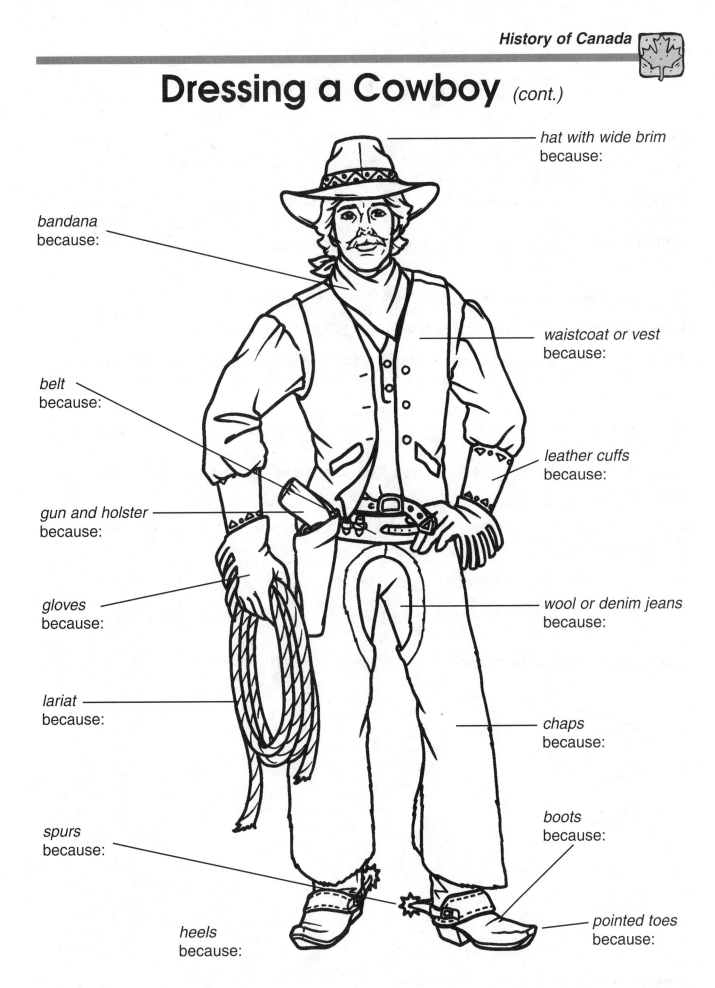

hat with wide brim
because:

bandana
because:

waistcoat or vest
because:

belt
because:

leather cuffs
because:

gun and holster
because:

gloves
because:

wool or denim jeans
because:

lariat
because:

chaps
because:

boots
because:

spurs
because:

pointed toes
because:

heels
because:

Dressing a Cowboy *(cont.)*

Answer Key

hat: wide brim kept the sun out of his eyes; carrying water (ever hear of a ten-gallon hat?); keeping things important (ever hear of "keep it under your hat)?"; keeping things in the hatband; in rain and snow it was a little umbrella; protected the head from heat, sun, and cold; fanning fires; as a pillow

bandana: keep dust out of the mouth and nose; clean things; wipe sweat; bandage; tourniquet; protect neck from sun

waistcoat or vest: added warmth; protection from burrs and thorns

leather cuffs: protection from thorns and animal bites

gloves: to protect hands from rope burns and reins; protections from sun; protection from animal bites and working with barbed wire fences

lariat: needed to catch cattle, horses and other animals; roping for entertainment and skill

belt: holds pants up; can be an extra rope when needed

gun, gun belt, and holster: personal protection; hunting; gun belt holds extra bullets

wool or denim jeans: long-wearing materials; warm

chaps: protect the legs when riding through brush; warmth; protection from rain, cattle horns animal bites; cushion the knees when working on the ground

spurs: used to prod the horse's thick, matted fur; decoration and status

boots: to protect the feet and lower leg; warmth; durability in difficult land; pointed toes allowed the boot to fit easily in the stirrup

high heels: to dig into the dirt while roping animals; to keep the foot in the stirrup

Royal Canadian Mounted Police

One of the most famous police forces in the world is the Royal Canadian Mounted Police. People all over the world recognize their bright red coats and their beautiful horses. This distinctive group of men and women police all of Canada except Ontario and Quebec, and the force numbers more than 14,000 "Mounties."

The first group of 275 men were known as the North West Mounted Police, and they began the force in Dufferin, Manitoba. Their goal was to head west to Fort Whoop-Up and several other forts in order to stop the illegal selling of whiskey to the people of the Blackfoot Confederacy. They set out for their 287 km (800 mile) trip in 1874. They arrived in southern Alberta in October.

The first men who joined came from different backgrounds, such as soldiers, teachers, students, artists, lawyers, farmers, etc. According to letters they wrote, they knew little about the vast territory to which they were headed. But these men had one common characteristic . . . they were seeking adventure.

The trip they made was called the great March West and was not well planned. They took moccasins, gloves, stockings, boots, horses, and food for their animals, but they didn't carry canteens. On their trip the men's shoes wore out, and they used sacks on their feet. But these rugged men made it to their destination to begin patrolling the wild Canadian frontier.

The whiskey trade in the western territories brought many problems. One serious problem was that the native people of the First Nation would trade much needed items for the drink instead of buying the practical items they needed, such as food, cooking pots, horses, and guns for hunting. Some of the native people who drank whiskey couldn't make good decisions and hurt other people or themselves. The result of the presence of the North West Mounted Police was that the Blackfoot people's conditions improved. The chiefs of the Blackfoot Confederacy liked the Mounties because when they made a promise to the native people, they would keep it.

Royal Canadian Mounted Police *(cont.)*

Another goal was to have one law for everyone. Often, whiskey traders thought they did not have to have the same laws towards the Native Americans. But this small group of men was successful in bringing peace to the territory and set standards for the men and women to follow.

Later, in the 1880s another crisis arose. The loss of the most important food source on the plain. Because of over hunting for their hides, the buffalo were nearly gone. The white hunters were entering the land of the Metis and First Nation People and many people were already starving. The Metis under Louis Riel and Gabriel Dumont and some Native American people fought to stop the "progress" of the settlers coming on their land. All sides lost lives in that war.

During the Klondike Gold Rush, the jurisdiction of the Mounties was extended to the Yukon. It was not an easy job keeping order with the gold-hungry prospectors pouring into the area.

In 1920 the name of the North West Mounted Police was changed to the Royal Canadian Mounted Police (RCMP).

The RCMP is also famous for the "Musical Ride." This famous event on horseback started in 1870 and was drawn by Frederic Remington in 1887 for *Harper's Weekly*. The striking all-black horses ridden by the Mounties in the event are specially bred in Ontario so that they will be the same size and color. Queen Elizabeth II has been given three of these horses as gifts. Their names are James, Burmese, and Centennial. The RCMP Musical Ride tour goes all over the world. They are good ambassadors for their country.

The Great March of the North West Mounted Police was reenacted in 1999 to commemorate the 125th anniversary of the founding of the force. The documentary of the event has a Website: *http://www.rcmpmarchwest.com*

Today the Royal Canadian Mounted Police only wear their red coats on special occasions, but this well-respected group of men and women is admired throughout the world.

The Royal Canadian Mounted Police *(cont.)*

Here are pictures of Royal Canadian Mounted Police officers to color. The uniform has changed many times over the years. You might want to investigate some of the older uniforms and draw pictures of them also. Use this guide to color the picture.

coat
bright red

hat
tan with a black band

pants
black with yellow stripes on the sides

boots
brown

belt
black

buttons
yellow

gloves
black

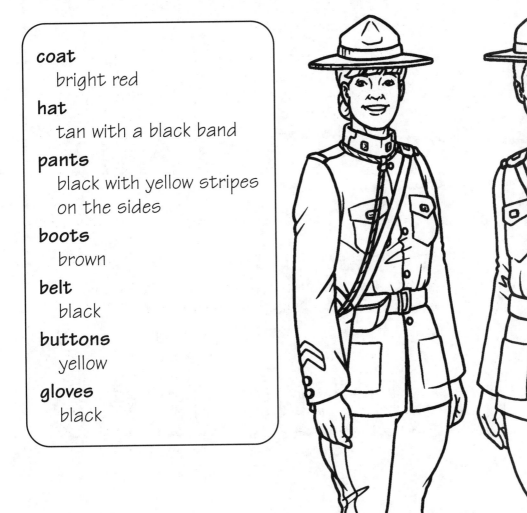

Language and Literature

A Land of Two Languages

Canada has a very strong history with France. In the early years, many explorers and settlers came to Canada from France. Much of eastern Canada was once part of the French empire.

When Canada became part of the British Empire in 1763, many people who had been French citizens kept their French traditions and their French language. This created many problems between French- and English-speaking people.

In 1969 the Canadian government passed The Official Language Act. This act made English and French both official languages of Canada. Official documents and legal matters are written in both languages. People who speak French are called *francophones*, and people who speak English are called *anglophones*.

The province of Quebec is almost entirely French speaking. Montreal is the second-largest French-speaking city in the world next to Paris, France. In Quebec the road signs and informational signs are all in French. If you do not know some French words, it can be difficult to get around Quebec.

Use pages 78 and 79 to make a little book that will help you learn some simple French phrases. If you enjoy learning these, maybe you would like to learn more in the future!

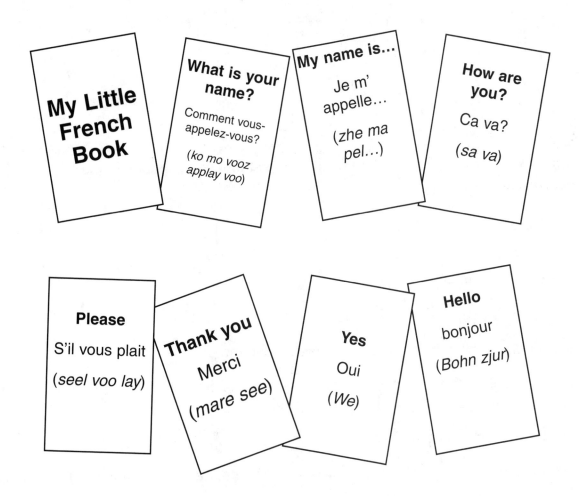

Language and Literature

French Word Book

Directions

1. Duplicate page 79.

2. Fold the page in half lengthwise and crease.

3. Fold in half widthwise, then fold again. Unfold completely. The paper will have eight sections.

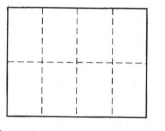 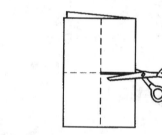

4. Refold along center fold widthwise. Have fold at top of paper. Cut along the vertical fold to the next horizontal fold halfway down. Unfold.

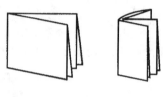 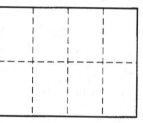

5. Refold lengthwise. Push ends together so that the center bows out on either side. Fold pages so that they all go in the same directions to make the pages of the book.

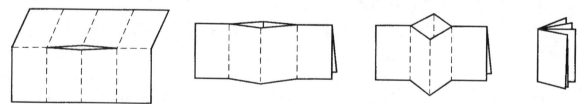

Suggested Activities

- Have students color the book and add pictures to the pages.

- You may want to have the students make their books out of plain paper and write the words on the pages along with their own pictures.

- Have the students practice saying words to each other.

- Have the students look up French words in a dictionary and make another book using their own words.

French Word Book

What is your name?

Comment vous-appelez-vous?

(ko mo vooz applay voo)

My name is...

Je m' appelle...

(zhe ma pel...)

How are you?

Ca va?

(sa va)

My Little French Book

Hello

bonjour

(Bohn zjur)

Please

S'il vous plait

(seel voo lay)

Yes

Oui

(We)

Thank you

Merci

(mare see)

79

The Polar Bear Son

Read *The Polar Bear Son* by Lydia Dabcovich.

This is an Inuit folk tale with very nice illustrations. Read the story to the students and share the pictures with them.

Discussion Questions

- In what ways was the polar bear a good son?

- How did he help the woman?

- Why did the townspeople want the bear to go away?

- Who warned the old woman?

- Why do you think the bear returned?

- Why would a polar bear be a good son to have in the Arctic?

- Why wasn't the old woman afraid to have a bear for a son?

Have the students make up a story in which someone has another animal for a son. What if someone had a dog for a son? Or a whale? What would the animals have to offer the people? What would the people have to offer the animals? Would where you live make a difference in the type of animals you would choose? Why?

Ask the students what it would be like to have an animal as a brother or sister? How would that change their lives? Which animal would they choose?

Have the students draw pictures of families with different animals in them and explain what life would be like for those families.

An Arctic Diorama

Suggested Reading: The *Polar Bear Son* by Lydia Dabcovich

Have your students look at the pictures in *The Polar Bear Son* for ideas to make their dioramas. If you do not have that book, use other pictures of the Arctic, its animals, and the Inuit way of life.

A diorama is like a little scene from a story. When people see your diorama, they should be able to tell what your story is about. Think of a little story you would like to tell about the Arctic and make your own diorama.

Materials

- a shoebox or other small box

- cardboard or construction paper

- white paper

- paper of other colors

- glue

- scissors

- crayons

- snow mixture (see recipe on page 111)

Directions

1. Cut the white paper to fit in the back sides of the inside of the box. Draw a line between the sky and earth and color the sky a light blue or gray. Add a few clouds and hills.

2. Make snow for ground cover (see recipe) and cover the bottom of the box. Make little hills and ridges in the snow. Let the snow dry.

3. Decide which figure you want to use from the next page or make your own.

4. Color the figures and cut them out.

5. Attach a small strip of construction paper or cardboard to the bottom back of each figure. Fold the base so each figure will stand up on the bottom of the box.

Hint: Add interesting things to your diorama. For instance, a small mirror makes a good lake. Add small sticks for a fire or fishing pole.

An Arctic Diorama (cont.)

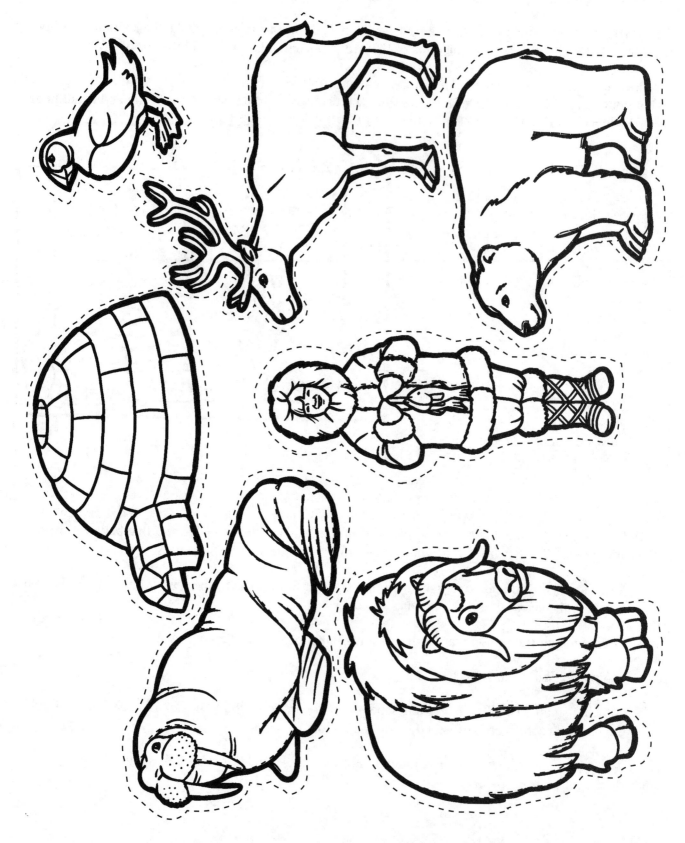

Mama, Do You Love Me?

Read *Mama, Do You Love Me?* by Barbara M. Joose, illustrated by Barbara Lavellee.

This Inuit folktale is illustrated with charming pictures. The story is about a little girl who asks if her mother would still love her under a series of unlikely circumstances. It is a wonderful tale for illustrating the dimensions of loving someone.

In the back of the book is a glossary of Inuit terms. The book also shows pictures of animals and items from the Inuit life. Notice the use of native symbolism in the background.

Discussion Questions

- Why do you think the little girl kept asking her mother how much she loved her?

- How would the mother feel if the girl broke the eggs?

- How would the mother feel if the girl poured water in the lamp?

- Can you be angry at someone and still love them?

- How would her mother feel if she ran away?

- What animals did the girl talk about turning into?

- Which animal was the mother most afraid of?

- Was there anything that the girl said that could stop her mother from loving her?

Explain to the children that *hyperbole* is a very large exaggeration. It is used to make a point. Have them locate examples of hyperbole in the story. A good example is on the page where the mother says, "I'll love you until the uniak flies into the darkness, till the stars turn to fish in the sky, and the puffin howls at the moon."

Have students make up their own examples of hyperbole and draw pictures to go with them.

Have students write stories about the person that they love the most. Encourage them to use hyperbole in the stories.

Anne of Green Gables

Background Information

The delightful series of the *Anne of Green Gables* books has charmed students since their first publication in 1908. The six books are set on Prince Edward Island and the descriptions and details allow the students to understand the beauty and serenity of life on that island in the early part of the twentieth century.

The main character of each book is Anne Shirley. The first book tells how Anne came to live on the island. She was an orphan who was sent to the island by mistake. Marilla and her brother Matthew Cuthbert had wanted a boy to come live with them and help work on the farm. It was common practice for orphans to be "taken in" in such a manner and for them to work for their keep. When Anne showed up instead of a boy, Marilla wanted to send her back, but Mathew convinced him that Anne should stay, and the little girl soon won their hearts and changed their lives forever.

The books follow the experiences of Anne as she grows from being a headstrong tomboy into a young woman who goes away to college and becomes a teacher on the island. It tells of her long courtship with Gilbert and their eventual marriage and life together. It is a series that chronicles her adventures of growing up and self discovery. Much of the story is based on the life of the author as she lived on the island, her experiences, the people that she knew, and her love of Prince Edward Island and its charm. The unpredictable and charming personality of Anne keeps the series alive and interesting for students of today.

Lucy Maude Montgomery was the author of the *Anne of Green Gables* series. Ms. Montgomery grew up on Prince Edward Island and captures the island life in her most famous series. She was born on November 30, 1874, in the town of Clifton. Lucy loved to read and devoured every book she could get her hands on. Even though few women of that time received higher education, Lucy attended both Prince of Wales College in Charlottestown on the island and later Dalhousie University in Halifax, Nova Scotia. She worked for a Nova Scotia newspaper, the *Halifax Chronicle,* and wrote for its evening edition. Later Lucy returned to Prince Edward Island to teach school for three years.

84

Anne of Green Gables *(cont.)*

Background Information *(cont.)*

When *Anne of Green Gables* was first published, it was a serial for a Sunday school paper. Serials were a very popular form of reading at the turn of the century, for books were expensive and many people read only the newspapers and other papers. The series became popular and lead to the next five books. The books are filled with positive values and the interesting, funny, sad, and entertaining experiences of Anne. The books in the series are *Anne of Green Gables, Anne of Avonlea, Anne of the Island, Anne of Windy Poplars, Anne's House of Dreams,* and *Anne of Ingleside.*

Lucy Maude Montgomery went on to write *Emily of New Moon* in 1923 and its two sequels, as well as *Pat of Silver Bush* in 1933 with one sequel.

Lucy married the Reverend Ewen MacDonald, a Presbyterian minister and moved to Toronto, Ontario. Although she left her beloved island, she said that she always returned to it in her dreams. She died in Toronto on April 24, 1942.

Suggestions

- You might want to read *Anne of Green Gables* aloud to your students during your unit on Canada. The book is full of positive values and has many themes to consider with your class.

- There are movies to accompany some of the *Anne of Green Gables* books. The stories were a television series on PBS Wonderworks and are produced by Sullivan Entertainment.

- Encourage the students to read all of the books in the series to follow the life of Anne and how she solved the problems she encountered.

- Discuss with the students how life is different today than it was in Anne's day. Then discuss how many of the problems that Anne faced are very relevant to life today.

Legends and Traditions

Totem Poles—Fact or Myth?

What is a fact? What is a myth? A fact is a true statement. It can be proven. A myth is a story that is not true. Sometimes myths are based on true stories, but over many years, the stories become exaggerated and untrue. It is important to know the difference between facts and myths.

What do you already know about totem poles? Before you start reading and studying about totem poles, try to decide whether the statements below are fact or myth.

1. Totem poles were carved from red cedar logs.

2. Native people used totem poles for a doorway, to support beams, or to hold a coffin of an important person in a hole at the top.

3. Totems were made by Native Americans all over Canada.

4. Totem poles were only made in the last 50 years.

5. To be the "low man on the totem pole" is not a good thing in the tribe.

6. If you put up a new pole, you would be expected to have a large feast and give everyone a gift for coming.

7. If one village had a larger pole, the next village would try to make theirs even larger.

8. The artists who carved the poles always signed their pieces.

Totem poles were never worshipped and they were not used to ward off evil spirits. They were erected to tell stories and to remember important historical events. They were for decoration, information, and prestige. The top of the pole usually carried the clan crest, often a raven, eagle, thunderbird, bear, beaver, orca, or frog.

Look for more information about totem poles on these Websites:

> *http://www.evergreen-washelli.com/text/totem_poles.html*

> *http://www.washington.edu/burkemuseum/nwtotem.html*

Hint: Fold this section under before reproducing.

Answers: 1. Fact **2.** Fact **3.** Myth – only about 6 tribes made totem poles **4.** Myth – they have been around since ancient times, but a drawing in 1791 is the earliest recorded of one. **5.** Myth – the order on the pole does not show one's importance. **6.** Fact – the feast was called a potlatch **7.** Fact **8.** Myth – most artists of older totem poles are unknown.

Legends and Traditions

Totem Pole Activity

Materials

- one cardboard tube from a roll of toilet paper per student

- markers or crayons

- spray paint or construction paper

- a yardstick or dowel/rod for every six or seven students

Directions

1. Students should choose a totem pole design that they like. Students may want to work in groups to come up with a theme for their totem pole.

2. Spray paint the tubes or cover them with construction paper.

3. Draw the animal or totem design on the tube.

4. Color with marker or crayon.

5. Have students connect their tubes together to form group totem poles. You will probably not want more than six or seven tubes in each totem pole. Slide the tubes over a yardstick or dowel/rod.

6. Stick the totem pole in a base of clay to display.

Some ideas to consider for the poles: whale, sea serpent, bear, beaver, wolf, frog, mosquito

You might want to group the totem poles by theme or have the students create a story from their group of totem sections. Totem poles can be used to illustrate stories the students have read.

Suggested Reading

Dramer, Pat. *Totem Poles: An Altitude Superguide.* Altitude Publishing, 2000

Indians of the Northwest. Gareth Stevens Publishing, 1997.

Keepers of the Totem. Time Life Books, 1993.

Jensen, Vickie. *Where the People Gather: Carving a Totem Pole.* University of Washington

Press, 1992.

Murdock, David. *North American Indian.* Alfred A. Knopf, 1995.

Mysterious Masks of the Northwest Coast

Masks had special significance to the Northwest Coast people. They were symbols for birds, animals, and supernatural beings. They were used for many ceremonial dances and theatrical performances. They represented their ancestors and the stories of their individual clans. Each family would use the masks to share their mythological figures of their heritage through song and dance.

One such special occasion when all types of masks would be used was the potlatch. This social event gave family members a chance to share their creative art through drama and song. The privilege of wearing a particular mask was handed down from one generation to the next.

The material that was carved was often red and yellow cedar. Try to bring a piece of cedar to class so that the students can smell its unique fragrance. Ask them if they know of other uses for cedar, such as closet lining or sachets.

The northern tribes Tlingit, Haida, and Tsimshiam painted their masks differently from the southern Kwakiutl who emphasized the sculpted shapes.

Find pictures of masks in these resources.

---

http://www.mala.bc.ca/www/discover/educate/posters/lauriec.htm (Kwakiutl masks)

http://www.coastalarts.com (great mask resource)

Indians of the Northwest. Gareth Stevens Publishing, 1997.

Keepers of the Totem. Time-Life Books, 1993.

Wyatt, Gary. *Spirit Faces: Contemporary Native American Masks from the Northwest.* Chronicle Books, 1995.

Talk about the way the mask makers designed their masks.

- Can you see any geometric shapes? Which ones?

- Are there curved lines? Angular lines?

- What colors do they see?

- Of red, black, white, blue, and green, which colors do they see the most of?

- How do the masks make them feel? Happy, sad, afraid, etc.

Making a Mask

Materials

- paper plates
- scissors
- markers or crayons
- yarn or ribbon for tying the plate

Directions

1. Students will need to find where their eyes and nose would be on their paper plates and cut out those shapes.

2. Use a pencil to create a simple design similar to what they have seen on other masks.

3. They may want to think about a certain animal they are trying to imagine themselves being.

4. Color the mask with bright colors.

5. Make holes for adding the string to each side.

6. Have the students wear their masks and tell stories about their animals.

7. Have the students write a small skit using the animals they have created.

8. Have the students talk about what animals they chose and why.

90

Clan Crest Hats

The people of the Northwest coast displayed their family crests on various handmade items such as poles, houses, clothing, blankets, and weapons, but one of the most treasured was the "clan crest hat."

Carved of cedar or woven from roots, these hats were decorated with animals or supernatural beings that represented the clan. It was worn by the chief on special occasions such as a potlatch. Special people were asked to take care of the headpieces. It was a privilege to be one of the caretakers for this prestigious headgear.

Thinking Problem

Can you think of any object in our society that is regarded in high esteem?

That represents something special to all of us?

That has rules to its care?

That is displayed on important occasions?

That is displayed in important places?

Can be handed down from one generation to another?

It is used to honor someone who served in the military?

Look at the pictures of clan crest hats on the following page. If you were going to design a hat for your family, what would it look like? Draw your idea for a hat in the space provided. share it with your friends. Be ready to explain why you chose the symbols that you did.

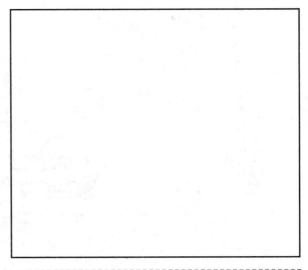

Hint: Fold this section under before reproducing.

Thinking problem answer: Our flag.

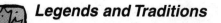
Clan Crest Hats *(cont.)*

Eagle

Wolf

92

The Potlatch

Imagine inviting someone to your birthday party and giving them your favorite and most expensive possessions! That is what the native peoples of the northwest coastal areas did at a potlatch.

The potlatch was a huge party where the host was expected to give extravagant gifts to his guests. A family would often work for a year to get ready to have a potlatch. Giving expensive gifts to the guests was a sign that the family was very wealthy and prosperous. For the Tlingit people, the word *potlatch* meant to give. A *potshatcl* was the Nootka word for gift.

Traditionally, it was a way for someone to honor a member of his or her family who died the year before and to give thanks to the family for funeral costs. Sometimes it was to show thanks for a new home or a decorated one. Other reasons for giving a potlatch would be important events such as a birth, marriage, etc. The Kwakiutl society is said to have given the most lavish potlatches. At a potlatch one would show respect to the spirits.

Guests would sometimes travel distances to attend the potlatches. They would always wear their best clothes. When the potlatch began, the guests' names and special titles would be announced and then they were seated according to their rank.

The potlatch ceremonies would last for many days and include many activities. There would be a time to remember the family member with songs and speeches. Next, you could count on an abundance of food. Guests were given gifts. The most popular item to receive was a Chilkat blanket. Other items included food, fur robes, cedar-bark mats, musical instruments, furniture, and even canoes.

Eating contests were part of the fun. Each family or clan tired to "out do" each other. Someone may even give the history of the food and the ancestral name for the dish. Dancing was another activity that the guests enjoyed.

The bigger the celebrations and the giving of gifts, the greater the honor of the host. In our terms, the host would be left penniless. A very wealthy man might give away all of his possessions except his house. But at a later time, he would be invited to other potlatches and the gift-giving would be even greater.

At one time, the tradition of the potlatch was against the law. The competition to give away expensive gifts was causing families to become poor.

Classroom Potlatch

Look at the list of famous Canadians (pages 11 and 12) and decide on a person to honor.

How do you think the invitations were sent for a potlatch? Decide on a time and a date for your potlatch and get the word out to everyone.

Look up information about the famous person that you have chosen to honor. Each student should write a nice thing to say about that person at the beginning of the party.

Have someone sing a song or play music. You can accompany the music with some drums. Do some dancing to the music. Try dancing in a circle.

Have students bring in food for the class. Find out if anyone has a food that has a story with it. For example, maybe someone likes a special type of cookie that his or her grandmother used to make. Have that student tell about the food as you eat it. What kinds of food do you think would have been served at a real potlatch?

Have an eating contest. You might want to have a timed contest instead of a "who can eat the most" contest. For example, you could see how fast someone could eat three saltines, then be able to whistle.

Finally, everyone should bring a gift to give to someone else. This can be a small thing, like a piece of candy or a pretty bead. See if you can give all of your gifts to other students in the class.

Your clan will be greatly honored by your potlatch success.

94

Arts, Crafts and Games

Maple Leaf Greeting Cards

The maple leaf is a symbol of Canada. It is so important to Canadians that they even put it on their flag.

Maple trees are used to make maple sugar and maple syrup.

Here are some projects you can do using maple leaf designs. If maple trees grow in your area, you can use the leaves for these projects. If you don't have any maple trees, use the stencils on the next page.

Materials

- a maple leaf stencil made of tagboard
- ink pads of various colors
- a small sponge
- a piece of card stock paper

Directions

1. Fold your card to make a note card. You can fold it at the top or along the left side.
2. Hold the stencil or leaf down firmly on the front of the card with one finger.
3. Press a small part of your sponge on the inkpad.
4. Rub the sponge over the leaf using outward motions.
5. Make sure that you go all around the leaf.
6. Remove your leaf and look at your design.
7. Experiment with different colors of ink.
8. Use different techniques with your sponge.

What does it look like if you swirl your sponge?

What happens if you combine colors?

What does it look like if you use a different sponge?

Write a nice message on the inside of your card and send it to someone special.

Other Uses for the Leaf Designs

- *Maple Leaf Print:* Use water colors and an old toothbrush. Lay your leaf or stencil on paper. Dip your toothbrush in the paint and spatter the paint over the top of it by pulling your finger across the bristles. Remove your stencil and see the design. Try using different colors.

- *Sun Print:* Put a leaf or stencil on a piece of colored construction paper and set in direct sunlight for an hour or more. Remove the leaf and you will be able to see the outline of the leaf on the paper.

Maple Leaf Stencils

Ukrainian Eggs—Not Just an Easter Tradition

Alberta is the home of the largest Easter egg in the world. It weighs 2,268 kg (5,000 lbs). It was created to honor the 100th anniversary of the formation of the Royal Canadian Mounted Police. The egg attracts thousands of tourists every year to the town of Vegreville, Alberta. It is even the center of a large annual festival!

There are many interesting facts about this egg.

The egg is gold, bronze, and silver in color and is made of permanently anodized aluminum. Its pattern is made up of 524 star patterns and 2,206 triangular pieces. There are 3,512 visible facets on the egg and 6,978 nuts and bolts hold it together. Inside the egg are 177 struts that hold it together on the inside.

The aluminum skin of the egg weighs 907 kg (2,000 lbs.). It is 7.8 meters (25.7 feet) long and
5.5 meters (18.3 feet) wide. The highest point from the ground is 9.6 meters (31.6 feet). It took over 12,000 man hours of design and fabrication to make this gigantic egg.

But what is the giant Ukrainian Easter egg doing in Canada? And what is Pysanky?

Pysanky are the geometric or symbolic designs that are created on egg shells. The tradition was brought to Alberta by the emigrants from the Ukraine in Europe. The making of Ukrainian eggs is a tradition with many families in the days before Easter.

For more than 2,000 years, the people of the Ukraine have decorated eggs. Before the introduction of Christianity, the eggs were also created during the long winter months to pass the time, ward off evil, and bring blessings for a good and fruitful spring. They decorated them believing that there were great powers in the egg. The egg symbolized the hope of life. It is easy to see why early Christians also used the egg to symbolize the resurrection of Christ.

Another tradition started by countrywomen and one which has been going on for centuries is the exchange of the eggs on Easter morning with friends and relatives. At other times the eggs are given like greeting cards as tokens of one's love. The different symbols on the eggs were made to fit the occasion whether it was a birth, wedding, illness, or even death.

Today gift stores carry the beautiful eggs for decorating and collecting.

The most fun, however, is in the making of the eggs.

Ukrainian Eggs—Not Just an Easter Tradition *(cont.)*

You can make Ukrainian eggs with your classmates and friends. And, once you try it, you will always appreciate them.

Begin by lightly sketching the design on the egg with a pencil. You may divide the egg in halves or quarters if you want the egg pattern to be symmetrical. Planning the pattern and the colors is very important.

You must use a special tool called a "kistka." The kistka is a stylus that holds the hot beeswax, which will be used to draw on the egg. A candle may be used to heat the metal head of the stylus, which is dipped into small block of wax to fill up the tiny funnel. By continually heating and dipping the stylus, the wax will flow as you move the tip across the pattern on the surface of the egg.

For example, if you want your background color to be yellow, then dip the egg in the yellow (or lightest color) first. Everything that you want to be left yellow must be covered with the wax. Then if you want to use orange, dip the egg into that dye and continue drawing with the kistka to save the orange part of the design. Then follow with your other colors in the order of their intensity. For example, use red, brown, and finally black.

Once the dying is finished, warm the egg over the candle flame to melt off the wax. Wipe the egg with a cloth to reveal the wonderful colors.

The egg is ready to varnish and place on a rack to dry.

The contents of the eggs can be removed before dyeing but do not need to be. The eggs can be blown out after the varnish has dried. Use a large needle to make a hole in one end of the egg. Make a slightly larger hole in the other end. Shake the egg or stir it with a needle to mix up the yolk. Blow through the small hole to force the contents out into a bowl. Rinse with water but make sure that you blow out the excess.

You can buy wax, kistka, dyes, and an egg pump from Ukrainian gift shops. One that has supplies available is The Ukrainian Gift Shop, Inc. (*www.ukrainiangiftshop.com*). Check the Internet to locate other resources.

Ukrainian Eggs—Not Just an Easter Tradition *(cont.)*

Encourage students to try learning about the symbols or creating their own designs. This can be done by giving them an egg pattern to trace.

Have the children choose one of the designs on the following pages. Next, they can divide the egg in sections. This is a good chance to talk about fractions. Students can use markers or crayons. Have them remember to start with the lightest color and use the black or darkest last.

If you do not want the students to work on eggs, they can use very heavy watercolor paper. Cut the paper into egg shapes. Use rubber cement and toothpicks. Have students write names or draw a simple design on the paper egg. Using egg dyes, dip, dry, and remove the glue. It's not as elegant as a Ukrainian egg, but it gives the idea of a resist process and dying is fun.

Tip: If you decide to let students try real eggs, use a hot glue gun. The result is not as delicate as the Ukrainina eggs, but it is easier.

Related Activities

If you do not want to do the eggs with your class, have them use the designs to make note cards or stationery. They can draw the designs to make a special message to someone.

Have your students find the Ukraine on a world map or globe. It is north of the Black Sea near Russia.

Visit these Websites for information about the World's Largest Easter egg and other pysanka information:

- *http://www.vegreville.com/tp2.html*

- *http://www.geocities.com/williamwchow/egg/e-egg.htm*

- *http://www.cuug.ab.ca:8001/VT/vegreville.html*

- *http://www.pysanka.com/*

Ukrainian Eggs—Not Just an Easter Tradition *(cont.)*

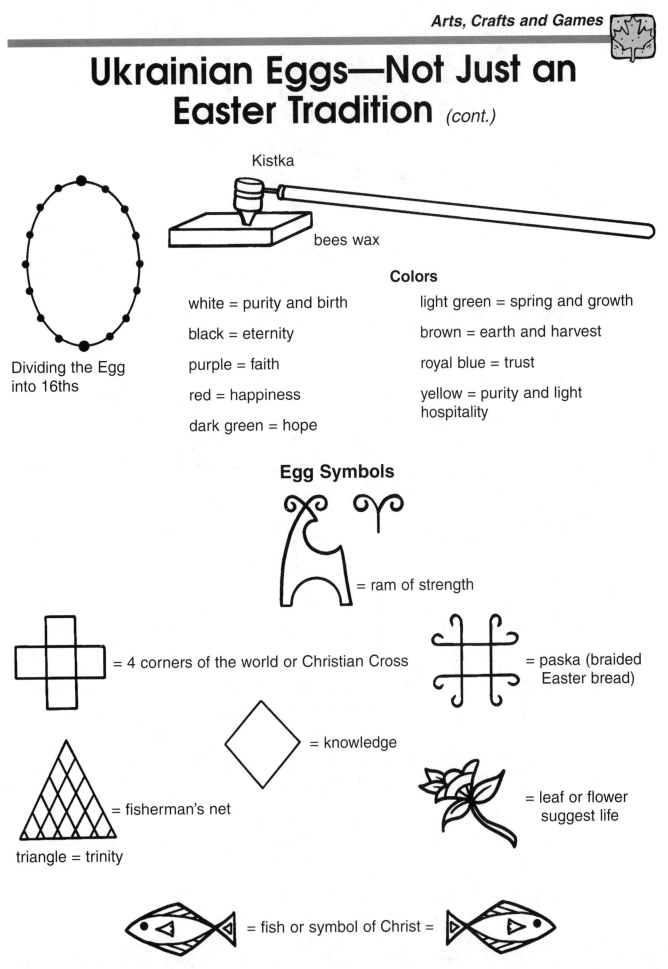

Kistka

bees wax

Dividing the Egg into 16ths

Colors

white = purity and birth

black = eternity

purple = faith

red = happiness

dark green = hope

light green = spring and growth

brown = earth and harvest

royal blue = trust

yellow = purity and light hospitality

Egg Symbols

= ram of strength

= 4 corners of the world or Christian Cross

= paska (braided Easter bread)

= knowledge

= fisherman's net

= leaf or flower suggest life

triangle = trinity

= fish or symbol of Christ =

Ukrainian Eggs—Not Just an Easter Tradition *(cont.)*

Egg Symbols

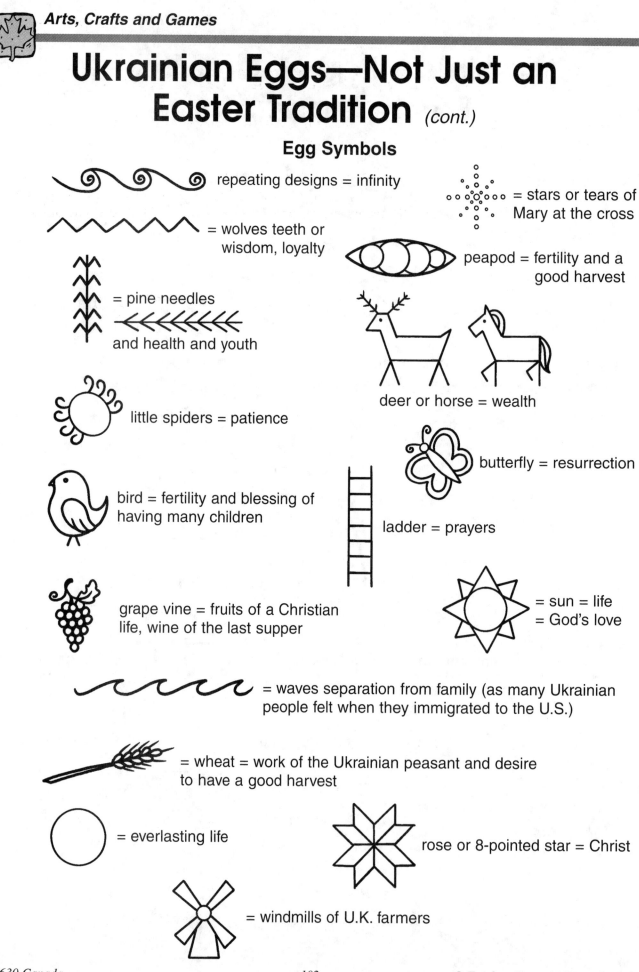

repeating designs = infinity

= wolves teeth or wisdom, loyalty

= pine needles

and health and youth

little spiders = patience

bird = fertility and blessing of having many children

grape vine = fruits of a Christian life, wine of the last supper

= stars or tears of Mary at the cross

peapod = fertility and a good harvest

deer or horse = wealth

butterfly = resurrection

ladder = prayers

= sun = life
= God's love

= waves separation from family (as many Ukrainian people felt when they immigrated to the U.S.)

= wheat = work of the Ukrainian peasant and desire to have a good harvest

= everlasting life

rose or 8-pointed star = Christ

= windmills of U.K. farmers

102

Inuit Art—Printing and Carving

The Inuit word for a carving is a "sinunguak" meaning "a small thing you make." Their word for a print is "titoraktok" meaning "marks you make with your hand."

According to James Houston, an artist who lived in the Arctic from 1948–1962, in *Confessions of an Igloo Dweller* there is no Inuit word for art, rather they consider "living in harmony with nature their art." Today, thanks to the initiative of Houston, the carvings, prints, and other crafts are sold at the Inuit-owned cooperatives.

Printing Activity

Examples of Inuit printing can be found in the work of Pitseolak. Refer to *Pictures Out of My Life* by Dorothy Eber.

Materials

- Styrofoam trays like the ones used for meat and vegetables in the grocery store
- pencils
- 2 ink brayers
- tubes of washable printing ink in red, blue, white, and yellow
- 3 cookies sheets (or something similar for rolling out the ink)
- lots of newspaper

Directions

1. Show students pictures of prints by Inuit artists. Discuss them.
   - What colors do they use?
   - What shapes do they use?
   - What is their subject matter?
2. You can approach this in two different ways.
   - Students can imitate the work of the Inuits.
   - The class can discuss how the artists' surroundings influenced their work. The students can create prints from their own environment.
3. Have students use the pencils to make their designs in the Styrofoam trays.
4. Roll the paint in very thin layers onto the trays. Do not get ink into the indentations.
5. Press the trays onto paper.
6. Let the students practice to get the technique down.
7. Have them tell stories about their prints.
8. Students can use their prints to make classroom pictures, greeting cards, or posters.

Soap Carving

Here's an activity that combines creativity and learning more about Inuit art. This is a project for older students who can handle a table knife or carving tools. You may just want to do a demonstration and let parents have the option of trying it at home.

Examples of Inuit carvings can be found in *The Inuit* (see the bibliography) and on these Websites:

- *http://www.culturel.org/NUNAVUT/*
- *http://www.inuitart.org/*
- *http://collections.ic.gc.ca/cape_dorset/indexl.html*
- *http://www.eclatart.com/Inuit_Art_Gallery_Enter.html*

Materials

- large bars of soap
- pencil
- carving knife or table knife
- potter's needle or large embroidery needle
- copies of the patterns on pages 105 and 106

Directions

1. Lay the bar of soap flat and the place pattern on top.

2. With a pencil, trace around the shape.

3. Repeat on the other side, being careful to line up the pattern closely to the other side.

4. Try to imagine the top, rear, and front of the animal and outline the areas to cut out.

5. Use the potter's needle or large embroidery needle for details such as fur, claws, eyes, etc.

6. Remove the excess soap by carving it out.

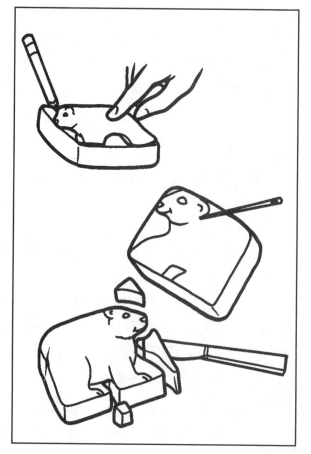

Another way to create a sculpture would be to use modeling clay or "Sculpty" and talk about the simple smooth shape.

If you watch the movie *Nanook of the North*, you will see that Nanook made an ice sculpture of a polar bear for his son.

Soap Carving *(cont.)*

Example

side

back

Side Patterns

bear

seal

walrus

musk ox

#3630 Canada

Soap Carving (cont.)

Side Patterns (cont.)

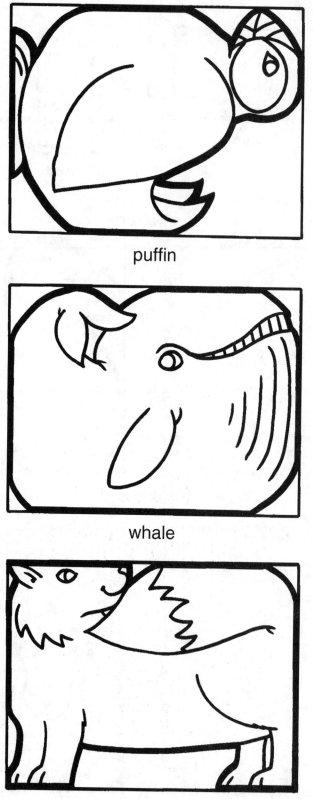

puffin

whale

sled dog

106

Chilkat Blankets—The Blankets That Tell Stories

Imagine having a blanket that took a year to make! That would make that blanket a very valuable possession, wouldn't it? The Chilkat blankets of the Northwest were highly prized possessions of the tribes in that area.

The Tsishiam tribe was the first to weave the Chilkat. Then another tribe of the Tlingits, the Chilkat, created their own unique designs. This is the group that gave the common name to the blankets. At first, only the rich or nobility could own one or make one. And, of course, it was a privilege to wear one.

Men would make the pattern, pattern boards, and looms. Their designs often told legends that only the designer could interpret. The geometric patterns of the blankets were often symbols used by the clan. Patterns taken from nature would include animal shapes and other natural forms. The symmetrical designs of animals often looked like they were cut down the center and laid out flat.

The men would also supply the goat skin. The women would take the wool off the hide, card it, and roll two strands together to make a stronger thread. The women also collected the natural ingredients to make the dyes: cedar bark, moss, bugs, and lichen. The yarns would be boiled in copper or urine to increase the color. The traditional colors were yellow, dark brown, and greenish-blue.

The loom was simple with two standing poles and a cross bar. Stones were used to weigh the small bundles of yarn, which the women would weave in and out of the warp using only their fingers.

Dance aprons were the first pieces made in the style. Later came blankets, leggings, purses, and tunics. Besides wearing the Chilkat blankets at the special potlatch ceremony, they were also proudly displayed outside of a gravehouse while the body was laid in state.

Chilkat Blankets—The Blankets That Tell Stories *(cont.)*

The Chilkat story of its origin says that long ago a Tsimshian women lived on the Skeena River in British Columbia. She was a widow from the village of Kitkatla. She lived with her only daughter who was named Hi-you-was-clar (Rain Mother). It was a very bad time in the village when the winter snows were deep and the people were hungry. The daughter sat day after day in a hungry stupor, staring at the intricately carved and painted picture that covered the back wall of their house. Although they were poor, they were from a once rich and proud family. The picture on the back wall took possession of the girl. She could not stop thinking about it and set up a rude framework loom where she lost herself in the desperate determination to weave an apron of the same design. She forgot her hunger in the work. She made the first Chilkat design apron. Later she was betrothed to the son of a chief and her father-in-law was greatly honored by her gift.

Use this reference: "The Chilkat Blanket" by George Emmons at this Website:

http://alaskan.com/docs/blanket.html

Tips to Remember When Making Your Own Chilkat Blanket

- Be sure to leave a wide margin around the design to add fringe later.

- Plan your colors and use the crayons to begin coloring. Remember that the colors of the Chilkat would be colors from natural dyes: yellow, dark brown, and greenish-blue. But let your imagination work on the design.

- Cut fringe around the bottom edge.

- Fold the blanket at the shoulders to hang on the line to display around the room.

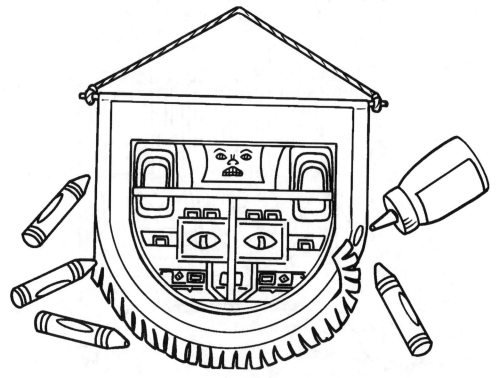

Chilkat Blanket Activities

Here are some activities related to Chilkat blankets.

Explore pictures of the Chilkat blanket in these references or on the Internet.

- Murdoch, David. *North American In dian.* Alfred A. Knopf, 1995.

- *Indians of the Northwest.* Gareth Stevens Publishing, 1997.

Discussion Questions

1. Why do you think it took so long to make a Chilkat blanket?
   - Goat hair would require more time to prepare than lambs wool; using the hand loom; the intricate patterns involved in blanket designs
2. Name some geometric patterns.
3. Why do you think the patterns were geometric?
   - Some were symbols used in their clan. Geometric patterns are easier to weave.

Dyeing Experiment

Have the children bring in plants, vegetables, and nuts local to your region.

Boil the materials separately.

Dip undyed strips of wool or scraps of white cotton into the water. Have the students tell which ones they like.

Make a chart of the colors they make. Display the chart for the classes to see.

Make a Chilkat Blanket

Materials: manila paper (this will represent the warp which was never dyed); crayons; scissors

Directions

1. After looking at pictures of the blankets, have students design their own by choosing a few geometric shapes, a symbol that means something special to them (heart, flag, cross), or an animal that they would like to be.
2. Trace the patterns of a Chiltak onto paper.
3. Use a pencil and a ruler to divide the blanket into sections.
4. Cut out the patterns and trace around them on the paper.
5. Draw in other shapes.
6. Use a compass or, if you don't have one, use the lid of something in the room to trace around.

Sample Chilkat Blanket

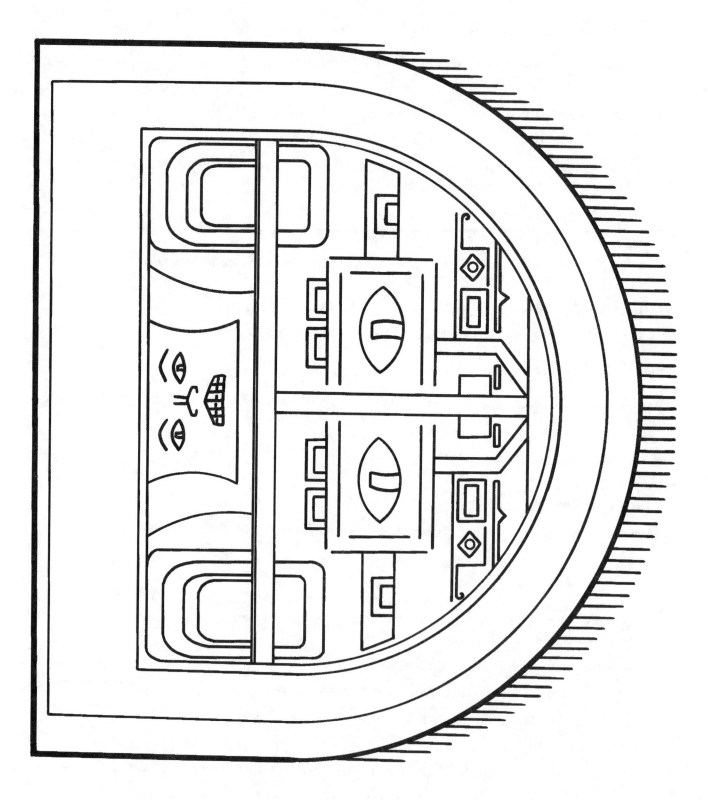

Let It Snow!

Much of Canada is covered with snow and ice many months of the year. The Canadians do not let cold weather, snow, and ice get in their way. They find ways to enjoy these winter conditions. They use snow for many sports such as skiing, snowmobiling, and sledding. They use ice for games such as hockey and curling. They also use ice and snow to make beautiful sculptures and even castles.

You can make your own snow to use to create snow sculptures, igloos, and dioramas of Arctic life. Here are two easy recipes to use.

Materials: powdered laundry detergent; water; waxed paper

Directions for Snow for Sculptures

Mix two cups of laundry detergent and 59 mL (1/4 cup) of water.

Stir until you have a thick, clay-like substance. If it is too thick, add a little more water but be careful only to add a little at a time so your clay is not too runny.

Mold the clay into shapes. You can make polar bears, birds, igloos, or anything that your imagination can come up with.

You will have to work quickly, as this clay will dry very soon.

Put your creations on waxed paper and in only a couple of hours they will be dry enough for you to enjoy.

Directions for Snow for Ground Cover

Mix 1 cup of laundry detergent and 59 mL (1/4 cup) of water.

This mixture is runnier and can be used to cover cardboard to create a snowy-looking ground or background. This will take a little longer to dry. When it is dry, sprinkle it with a little dry laundry detergent to make it look like freshly fallen snow.

Use small mirrors or pieces of aluminum foil to represent frozen lakes and ponds.

Make Your Own Snow Goggles

Snow blindness is a very dangerous and painful condition. It is caused by the bright springtime sun reflecting off very white snow. In Nunavut and other areas, snow blindness is a real danger.

The Inuits had a clever way of preventing snowblindness before sunglasses and goggles were invented. They made their own snow goggles from antler and sinew. The antlers came from caribou and the sinew are small muscle fibers taken from either the caribou or other animals that are hunted for food.

How did their goggles work? They would cut tiny slits in pieces of antler and tie the antlers to their faces with the sinews. The tiny slits would only let in small amounts of light and would keep out a lot of the brightness. To keep out even more bright light, the Inuits would cover the antlers with charcoal ashes.

Make your own snow goggles and try them out for yourself. It does not have to be snowing. You can try them on any sunny day. Be careful never to look at the sun even with snow goggles or sunglasses. Looking directly at the sun can damage the retina of your eyes and damage your sight forever!

Experiment with your goggles.

Make the eye slits very skinny at first. Try making them a little bigger, then a little bigger and see which size works best for keeping out the sunlight.

Make your goggles out of light-colored paper and try them. Color the goggles a darker color and see if you can tell the difference.

Lay two pieces of paper on the ground or a table outside in the bright sunlight. One piece of paper should be white. One piece of paper should be black or very dark. Look at both sheets while wearing your goggles. Can you tell which sheet of paper reflects the most light? Can you see how snow blindness would be a problem for people living in the Arctic?

What are the problems that you have when you wear the snow goggles? How could snow goggles cause problems for people who go out hunting? What kinds of dangers would there be for people wearing snow goggles?

Why are sunglasses and modern goggles better than the antler snow goggles? Why didn't the Inuits use sunglasses?

Snow Goggles

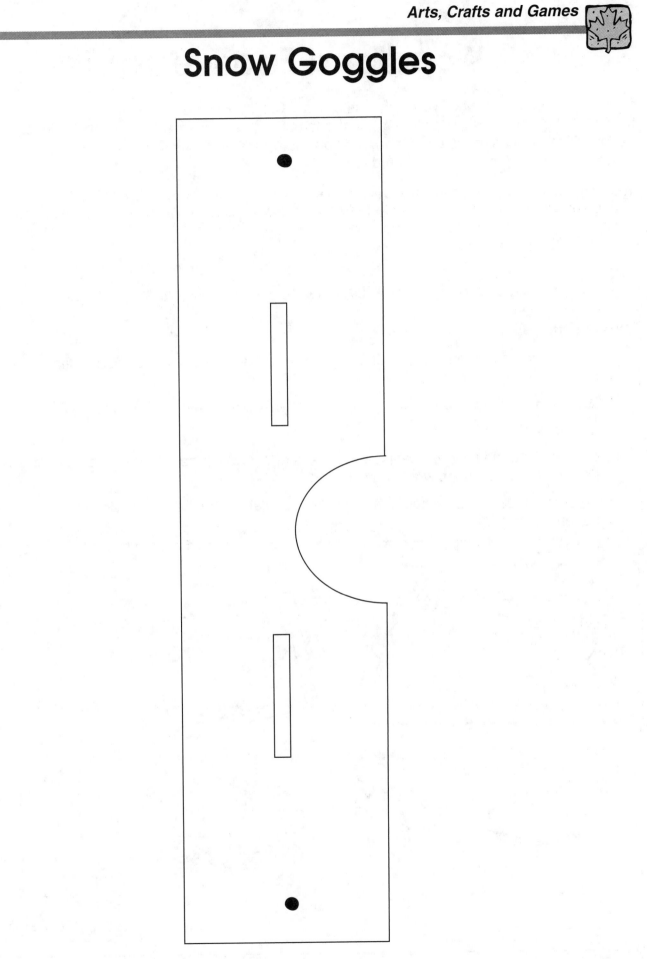

Woodland Footwear

The Native Americans who lived in the cultural area of the Eastern Woodlands needed footwear when they were hunting through the forests. Moccasins were the shoes of these people. The moccasins were soft and quiet but were durable and strong. Moccasins were made of tanned animals hides, often deerskin.

You can make your own moccasins very easily.

Materials

- felt
- yarn or heavy thread
- scissors
- large needle
- glue
- decorative items

Directions

1. Enlarge the pattern on the following page until your foot will fit in the middle with at least 10 cm (4 inches) in front of your toes and behind your heel.

2. Cut out the pattern and sew the heel and toe where indicated by the stitching lines.

3. Fold down the cuff.

4. You can decorate your moccasins with beads or colored thread. Look up some designs that the woodland tribes would have used.

5. Wear your moccasins for bedroom slippers. You can make them to give to your family for presents!

Woodland Footwear

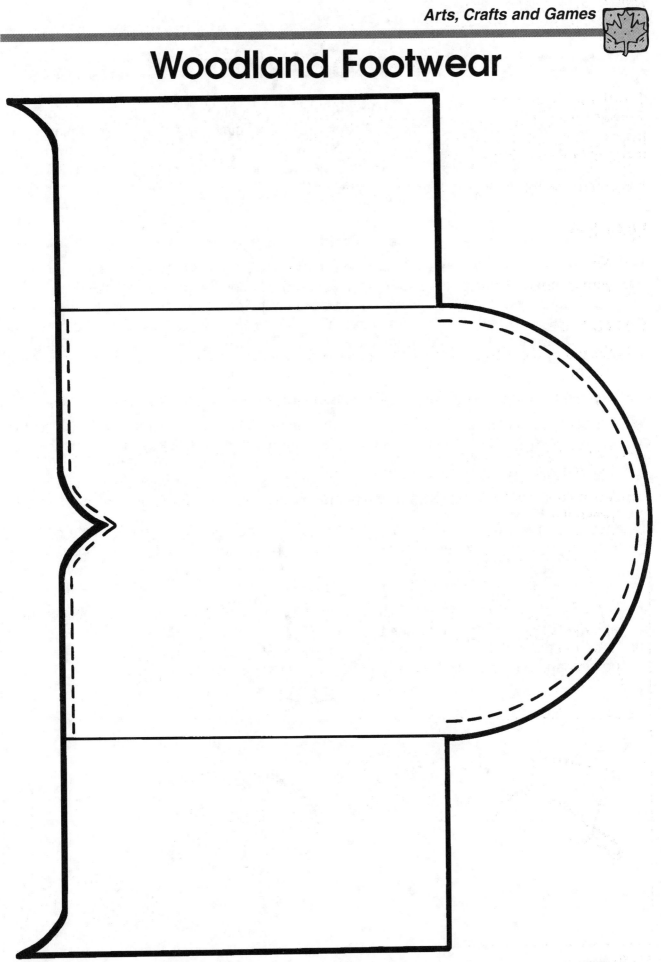

Fun Indoor and Outdoor Games

People everywhere like to play games. When the cold, dark nights set in at the Arctic, people like to have ways to amuse themselves. Another reason to play games is to enjoy being outdoors on sunny days. What other reasons do people have for playing games? How many of these games seem familiar to you? Do you play any that are like these games from the North? What do you call your games? Read the descriptions of these Canadian Games to see if you would have liked to played them.

Cat's Cradle: Inuit

This string game is played with a long cord made of sinew. The first player twists the cord around the fingers of both hands and makes a pattern that could represent a lake, igloo, mountain, or animals. Then the second player picks up the cord and makes another figure. This game was played night after night in the igloo. It was ideal for passing time in a crowded igloo. An elderly person may wait to the very end to show his or her complicated figure last and impress the audience.

Bones: Inuit

First, carve small animals and people from the bones of seal flippers for this game. Divide the set of bones equally between two people on a fur mat. Each player picks a bone and holds it above the mat and lets it drop. The one that lands right side up wins. The losing bone is laid aside. The player with the winning bone drops his or hers while the other picks up a new one. The game is finished when one player has no bones left.

Another variation would be to throw all the bones up and see how many land with the carved figures standing up or facing the player. The player with the most upright pieces wins.

The Toss Game: Inuit

Find one large piece of circular walrus skin. Have a group of friends hold onto a section while you get in the center. Everyone tosses the person in the center and makes the skin very taunt. The best is determined by who can be tossed the highest and not lose his or her balance and land on his or her feet. The game is often played with a blanket in place of the walrus skin.

Fun Indoor and Outdoor Games *(cont.)*

The Stick Game: Haida and Many Other Groups

This game has many variations. It usually involves a set of sticks. The sticks might be made of bone or wood. All of the sticks have markings except one, which is called the "bait." The players lay their sticks in front of them. One player takes the bait stick and several others. Under the cover of a cedar bark, that player shuffles the sticks into two or three bundles. He or she then lays the bundles out for the opponent to see. The opponent has to select the bundles where the bait is hidden to win. There were many variations of this game among many tribes throughout North America.

Spinning Tops: Inuit and Other Groups

The tops are made of wood with a pin in the center of a cylinder. A sinew string through the pin's center hole is wound so that it can be spun on the ice. Several people begin spinning their tops upon signal. The winner is the one whose top spun the longest.

Spinning Eskimo: Inuit

A piece of ice is made into a large top that is flat on the top for a man or child to sit. The point is placed into a small hole in the ice. The "victim" sits on top while two others spin him by using sticks. The object is to spin him around until he or she does not feel well.

Ball Game: Plains and Eastern Woodland Tribes

Each player has a long stick with a net on the end. The players form teams. The players try to catch or scoop a ball with their net and throw it to another player. The goal is to get the ball across the playing area into the other team's goal.

Ring-and-Pin Game: Inuit and Many Other Groups

This game is similar to cup-and-ball games. The "cup" is a carved bone (animal or other shape or figure) with several long, thin holes. A long, pointed stick is attached to the cup with a string. The object of the game is to throw the stick up and catch it in one of the holes. The player may need to catch the stick a certain number of times or in different holes in a particular order. If the player misses twice, he has to pass the cup to the next player.

Fun Indoor and Outdoor Games *(cont.)*

Hoop-and-Pole Game: Nootka

A 3.65-meters (12-foot) hoop is made with a core of grass wrapped in cedar. The hoop is then rolled along the ground and players try to throw spears through it without knocking it over.

Snow Snake Game: Plains and Woodlands Tribes

The snow snake is a long, spear-like pole designed to slide over ice and snow. The game requires throwing the pole to see how far it will go. Another variation is to try to throw the pole to have it land in a particular place.

Shuttlecock Game: Kawkiutl

Each player has a wooden paddle, called a "quemal" and the team has a shuttlecock called a "quemlaiu" made from a stick with three feathers tied to it. The players stand in a circle. The first player hits the shuttlecock up and to the right to the next player. The object is to keep the quemal in the air. The one who lasts longest wins.

Activities

1. Look at the pictures on pages 119 and 120. Match the pictures with the game descriptions above. Write the names of the games under the pictures.

2. Did you recognize any games that are like ones you know? Which ones? How are they like your games? How are they different?

3. How did people make use of the things they had near them? What materials are used in making your games? Do you make your games, or do you buy them?

4. Try making one of the games described above. What would you need? How would you do it?

Hint: Fold this section under before reproducing.

Answers to Question 1

1. Ball Game
2. Toss Game
3. Spinning Tops
4. Cat's Cradle
5. Snow Snake Stick Game
6. Ring-and Pin-Game
7. Shuttlecock Game
8. Hoop-and Pole-Game
9. Bones
10. Stick Game
11. Spinning Eskimo

Fun Indoor and Outdoor Games *(cont.)*

1.

_____

2.

3.

_____

4.

5.

_____

6.

_____

Fun Indoor and Outdoor Games *(cont.)*

7.

_____

8.

_____

9.

_____

10.

_____

11.

_____

Flying Across the Ice

Ice hockey is a fast and exciting game. It is the most popular sport in Canada. Maybe Canadians enjoy hockey because it was invented there.

Ice hockey is the combination of three sports. It is similar to an old Irish game called "shinny," but it is played while ice skating and it uses rules similar to football! The players of ice hockey need to wear a lot of protection because the game can become very wild and dangerous.

No one is certain who first played ice hockey, but the most common belief is that it was played by soldiers at Kingston, Ontario, in the winter of 1855. The bored soldiers had to come up with a sport that could be played in the cold climate of Canada so they adapted the old Irish game of shinny to the ice. The first recorded game of ice hockey was played in 1875 in Montreal, Quebec.

The current set of rules for the game is called the McGill Rules. These rules were established in 1879 to make the game suitable for competition.

The most famous prize for professional hockey is the Stanley Cup. This award is given every year to the best hockey team. The prize is a large silver cup, and it was first given by a man named Lord Stanley in 1893.

People of all ages play hockey in Canada. There are many amateur leagues and students play hockey in school.

Many of the most famous players of hockey came from Canada. Wayne Gretzky was born in 1961 in Ontario. He played for professional teams in Canada and the United States and has held almost every record in the National Hockey League. He retired in 1999. During his career he made 894 goals and 1,963 assists.

Other famous hockey players from Canada included Bobby Orr, Jean Beliveau, and Gordie Howe.

National Hockey League Teams from Canada

Eastern Conference	Western Conference
Montreal Canadiens	Calgary Flames
Toronto Maple Leafs	Edmonton Oilers
Ottawa Senators	Vancouver Canucks

Bonus Activities: Choose a hockey player that you admire and write a report.

Make a list of all of the teams that have won the Stanley Cup. How many of them were Canadian?

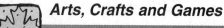

Lacrosse

Lacrosse is the national game of Canada. This game has a French name, but it is based on a game played by the Algonquin Indians and other native tribes.

The Native Americans called the game baggataway. It was a game of tribal warfare. Often as many as 500 men on each side would play the game. They would play the game for days at a time. Sometimes it was played by people from the same village. Other games would involve rival tribes that played the game in dangerous matches where people were injured or even killed.

Many of the French and English settlers who came to Canada were interested in the game of lacrosse. The native people enjoyed demonstrating their sport, but they had to limit the playing field for the spectators. In this way lacrosse changed from a roving chase to an ordered game.

The Europeans were interested in learning to play the game so rules and regulations came into existence to make it easier to learn. In 1856 the Montreal Lacrosse Club was formed. In 1861 the game was still being played with 25 men on a side. In 1867 definite rules for the game were written by the newly-formed National Lacrosse Association, and the number of players was limited to 12 men on a side. This was also the year lacrosse was officially adopted as the national sport of Canada. In 1933 the rules changed the number of players from 12 on a side to 10.

Lacrosse today is played by men and women, although the rules differ slightly. A men's team consists of 10 players: three defensemen, three midfielders, three attackmen, and one goalkeeper. The game is divided into 15-minute quarters. Women's lacrosse is played with teams of 12 members. The game is divided into 25-minute halves with a 10-minute break between. The size of the women's field is not written in the rules, but it is usually about 10 yards wider and 10 yards longer.

On the next page is a diagram of a regulation men's lacrosse field at the beginning of a game.

Examine the diagram and answer these questions.

1. How far is it from the end of the field to the middle? _____
2. How far is the net from the end of the field? _____
3. Which position is standing in the wing area? _____
4. Which position stands directly in front of the goal? _____
5. Which members of the opposing team get to stand in front of the goals? _____
6. How far is it from the net to the center line? _____
7. What is the length of the sides of the goal area? _____

Hint: Fold this section before reproducing.

Answers

1. 50 meters (55 yds.)
2. 13.7 meters (15 yds.)
3. midfielder
4. goalkeeper
5. attackmen
6. 36.5 meters (40 yds.)
7. 22 meters (35 yds.)

Lacrosse Playing Field Diagram

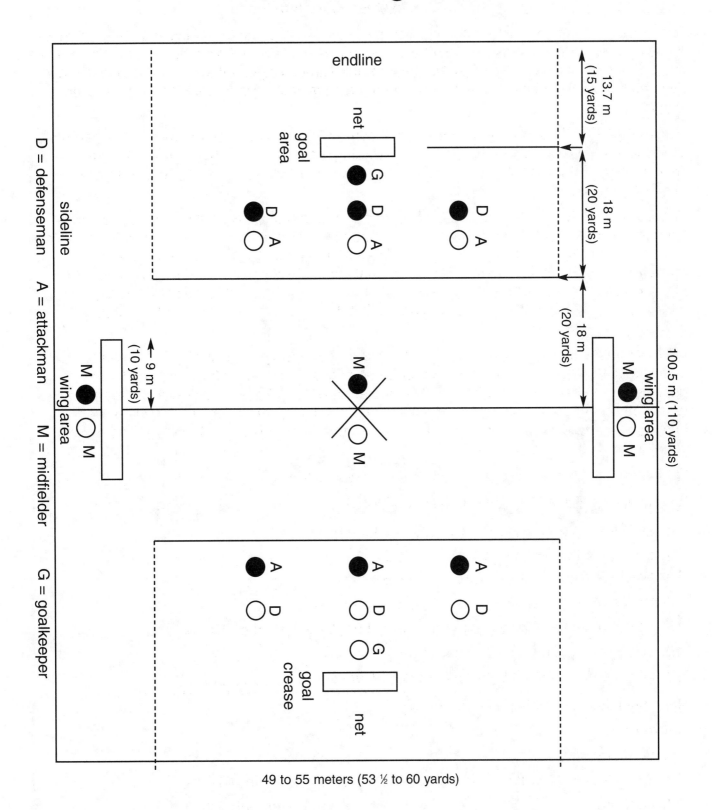

Food and Festivals

National Holidays

These are the national holidays celebrated in Canada. How many of the holidays are the same as ours? Which ones are different? What do you think Boxing Day is? *Hint:* It's the day after Christmas. What do boxes have to do with Christmas?

January 1—New Year's Day

March/April—Good Friday

March/April—Easter Monday

Third Monday in May—Victoria Day

July 1—Canada Day

First Monday in September—Labor Day

Second Monday in October—Thanksgiving

December 25—Christmas Day

December 26—Boxing Day

Boxing Day is the day after Christmas, December 26. Boxing Day used to be a day when people would give money to servants and tradespeople. On Boxing Day, people would put old clothing into boxes and take them to the poor people. Parents would give small gifts to their children, such as oranges, socks, and handkerchiefs. This was a tradition that began when Queen Victoria was the Queen of England.

Today, many people and organizations follow the Boxing Day tradition by giving to the poor during the Christmas holidays.

In Canada, government offices are closed on Boxing Day. Families spend this day enjoying each other's company and giving gifts. Just like in the United States, many people go to the malls to shop and to exchange gifts on this day.

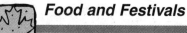

Canada—A Land of Festivals

Canadians are proud of their heritage and of their history. They love to share their pride with the world. During the year in Canada, there are many festivals, which celebrate the traditions and history of Canada. Here is a list of some of the many annual celebrations that you can attend throughout Canada. Discuss the names of the celebrations and talk about what you think they do there.

- **Festival Name:** Niagara International Music Festival

  Description: Music Festival for choirs, bands, and orchestras

  Date: beginning of July   **City:** St. Catharine's, Ontario

- **Festival Name:** Vancouver International Dance Festival

  Description: National and international dance companies combined with workshops in dance, films and discussion forums

  Date: March   **City:** Vancouver, British Columbia

- **Festival Name:** Winter Festival of Lights

  Description: An explosion of lights turns Niagara Falls and surrounding areas into a fairytale image.

  Date: November   **City:** Niagara Falls, Ontario

- **Festival Name:** Manitoba Livestock Expo

  Description: Manitoba's largest livestock show and sale and Manitoba Rodeo Cowboys Association Finals

  Date: first week of November   **City:** Brandon, Manitoba

- **Festival Name:** Celtic Colours International Festival

  Description: Celtic performers from around the world

  Date: October   **City:** Sydney, Nova Scotia

- **Festival Name:** Nova Scotia International Air Show

  Description: Featuring the Snowbirds Aerobatic Jet Team, the Sky Hawks Parachute Team, plus many more flying demonstrations

  Date: September   **City:** Shearwater, Nova Scotia

- **Festival Name:** Yukon Arts Festival

  Description: Home of the Klondike Gold Rush

  Date: September   **City:** Dawson City, Yukon

- **Festival Name:** Gatineau Hot Air Balloon Festival

  Description: Biggest balloon festival in Canada, up to 150 balloons of all colors and all shapes, 200 shows and activities

  Date: end of August   **City:** Gatineau, Quebec

- **Festival Name:** Festival by the Sea

  Description: More than 300 entertainers from across the nation gather in Saint John to celebrate Canadian music, dance, and culture.

  Date: August   **City:** Saint John, New Brunswick

Canada—A Land of Festivals *(cont.)*

- **Festival Name:** Montreal International Celtic Festival
  Description: The history of the ancient Celts and their legacy to Canadians of all origins
  Date: August   **City:** Verdun, Quebec
- **Festival Name:** Royal St. John's Regatta
  Description: North America's oldest organized sporting event, going strong at 183 years
  Date: August   **City:** St. John's, Newfoundland
- **Festival Name:** Frog Follies
  Description: Frog Follies, one of Manitoba's longest running summer festivals and the Canadian National Frog Jumping Championship
  Date: August   **City:** St. Pierre-Jolys, Manitoba
- **Festival Name:** Canada's National Ukrainian Festival
  Description: Canada's National Ukrainian Festival—features music, dancing, cultural demonstrations, workshops, and competitions
  Date: August   **City:** Dauphin, Manitoba
- **Festival Name:** Buffalo Days Exhibition
  Description: The Provincial Exhibition
  Date: July   **City:** Regina, Saskatchewan
- **Festival Name:** Festival of Flight
  Description: Celebrate Gander's unique aviation history
  Date: July-August   City: Gander, Newfoundland
- **Festival Name:** PEI Potato Blossom Festival
  Description: This festival revolves around the potato and the industry
  Date: July   **City:** O'Leary, Prince Edward Island
- **Festival Name:** Head-Smashed-In Buffalo Days Pow-Wow and Tipi Village
  Description: Aboriginal dance and drumming competitions as well as a traditional tepee village
  Date: July   **City:** Fort Macleod, Alberta
- **Festival Name:** Edmonton's Klondike Days
  Description: There is something magical happening at Edmonton's Klondike Days.
  Date: July   **City:** Edmonton, Alberta
- **Festival Name:** Banff Arts Festival 2002
  Description: For more than 70 years, an intensive three-week period of incredible events and entertainment
  Date: July-August   **City:** Banff, Alberta
- **Festival Name:** Festival Acadien de Clare
  Description: Canada's largest and oldest annual Acadian cultural festival
  Date: July   **City:** Clare, Nova Scotia

Canada—A Land of Festivals (cont.)

- **Festival Name:** Shakespeare By The Sea Festival

  Description: The Shakespeare By The Sea Festival is the longest-running outdoor summer theatre event in the St. John's area.

  Date: July-August   **City:** St. John's, Newfoundland

- **Festival Name:** The Yukon International Storytelling Festival

  Description: Each year, storytellers from around the world gather beneath the midnight sun on the banks of the legendary Yukon River.

  Date: May-June   **City:** Whitehorse, Yukon

- **Festival Name:** Stratford Festival

  Description: World class theatre running in repertory

  Date: April-November   **City:** Stratford, Ontario

- **Festival Name:** Yukon Quest International

  Description: Over 40 of the top mushers and sled dog teams from around the world compete in the toughest sled dog race in the world!

  Date: February   **City:** Whitehorse, Yukon

- **Festival Name:** Festival du Voyageur

  Description: The Festival du Voyageur is Western Canada's largest winter festival, recalling the great fur trade era when voyageurs explored the heart of Canada some 300 years ago.

  Date: February   **City:** Winnipeg, Manitoba

- **Festival Name:** Mr. Christie Quebec Winter Carnival

  Description: Considered like the world's largest winter carnival; lasts 17 consecutive days.

  Date: February   **City:** Quebec, Quebec

- **Festival Name:** Great Northern Arts Festival

  Description: Each summer, the town of Inuvik, Northwest Territories hosts the Great Northern Arts Festival: a phenomenal 10-day gathering of artists and performers from across the arctic and beyond.

  Date: July   **City:** Inuvik, Northwest Territories.

Have you ever been to any festivals like these? What was it like? Tell your classmates about your experiences. Why do people have festivals? What festivals are there in your town, or state? Have you ever been to a country fair or a state fair?

After you have discussed some of the festivals, choose one that you think is interesting. Find out more about that event. Write a report to share with your class.

Plan a trip to your event. Find it on the map. How would you get there? What would you take with you? What do you think you would learn about at your festival?

Make a poster for one of the festivals. Show pictures of what you would expect to see there. Try to get people to want to attend your festival.

The Calgary Stampede–A Taste of the "Old West"

Over a million people go to Calgary, the capital of Alberta, in July. Why do so many people visit there? They go to spend 10 days at one of the greatest outdoor shows in the world.

The Calgary Exhibition and Stampede is a ten-day extravaganza of rodeos, music, food, dancing, cattle roping, chuck wagon racing, and agricultural shows. During this incredible festival, the atmosphere is like the Old West. People dress in cowboy clothing and eat cowboy food. Prizes are given for cattle, horses, and other livestock. Farmers proudly compete for the highest awards in agriculture. Native Americans proudly dress in their traditional clothing and ride in the parade. Pancake breakfasts and hot air balloon races are part of the spectacle. The rodeo that is held there offers the largest prizes in the world for rodeo events.

One of the central events of the Stampede is the Chuck Wagon Race where chuckwagons race madly around a half-mile track. The action is wild and furious, much like the chariot races of ancient Rome.

The Calgary Exhibition and Stampede has a long history dating back to 1886. The main purpose of the Exhibition was to promote agriculture in Alberta and to give ranchers and farmers the chance to display their livestock and crops. The Stampede was added in 1912. Since then the festivities have grown from six days to ten days with the attendance first passing 1,000,000 in 1976. In 2000 the attendance reached 1,218,851. The show requires year-round planning by more than 2,000 volunteer helpers.

Here are some important dates in the history of the Calgary Exhibition and Stampede.

1884—Agricultural Society formed

1886—First Calgary Exhibition held

1912—September 1912, the first Calgary Stampede was held

1922—Calgary Industrial Exhibition held

1923—The Stampede hosted the first competitive Chuck Wagon Races

1932—The Calgary Exhibition joined with the Stampede to become the Calgary Exhibition and Stampede

1968—The Stampede becomes a 10-day event

1976—Stampede attendance surpasses one million for the first time

1982—The "Half-Million Dollar Rodeo" was introduced

1998—75th Anniversary of Chuck Wagon Racing at the Calgary Stampede

The Chuck Wagon— The Cowboy's Kitchen

Chuck wagons were important vehicles in the West. These sturdy little wagons carried food and supplies on cattle drives and for the ranch hands. The first chuck wagon was designed by Charles Goodnight in 1866. He took an old army wagon and adapted it to the needs of the trail cook.

The chuck wagon carried extra water in large barrels that were roped to the side of the wagon. Lamps, ropes, and large kettles were hung around the sides and underneath the wagon. In the bed of the wagon, the cook stored the supplies needed for tail cooking. Facing the back of the wagon was the "chuck box," a chest of drawers that held the essential food so the wild animals couldn't get to it. The tailgate of the wagon folded out to make a workspace and table for the cook.

Food on the trail was pretty boring. Even though the cowboys were herding thousands of cattle, the main meat that they had to eat was usually bacon, which they called "sowbelly." They also had beans and fried bread. The cooks would often try to spice up the meals by catching small animals on the prairie such as jackrabbits and prairie chickens. Large animals such as antelope were a prize for the hungry cowboys.

In July during the Calgary Stampede, there is a very exciting Chuck Wagon Race where chuck wagons are driven around a half-mile track at breakneck speeds. The event draws huge crowds and creates a lot of excitement. It has been going on since 1923. The 75th anniversary of the Chuck wagon Race was in 1998. How old will it be this year?

130

Make Your Own Chuck Wagon

Teacher's Note: The chuckwagon patterns should be copied onto lightweight tagboard. If that is not available, then the patterns will need to be pasted to lightweight board to give the wagon bottom, the wheels, and the axles the appropriate strength. The top can be made from regular white paper.

You can make your own chuck wagon by using the patterns on the following pages.

Directions

1. If you want to color your wagon, it is best to do that before you cut it out. Use crayons or markers to make the wagon look like it is made of wood. The top of the wagon would have been made of canvas. Remember that many of the wagons were old and dirty because of the hard use on the trail.

2. Carefully cut out the pattern pieces.

3. Work on the wagon bottom first. Fold along all of the dotted lines. Put paste or glue on the small flaps and stick them to the backs of the pieces that they line up with. The front of your wagon has a seat that sticks out.

4. Attach the axle pieces to the bottom of the wagon. Fold them down on the dotted lines.

5. Attach the center of the wheels to the axles where the small dots are. Use brads to hold the wheels and axles together.

6. Cut out the top of your wagon. Gently roll the top so that it forms a small tube. Let it unroll. Now it will be easier to attach to the top to the sides of the wagon. You can glue it underneath, or you can attach it with small pieces of double-sided tape or small tape rolls.

Now you are ready for the trail!

     #3630 Canada

Chuck Wagon Templates

front

Fold on
dotted lines.

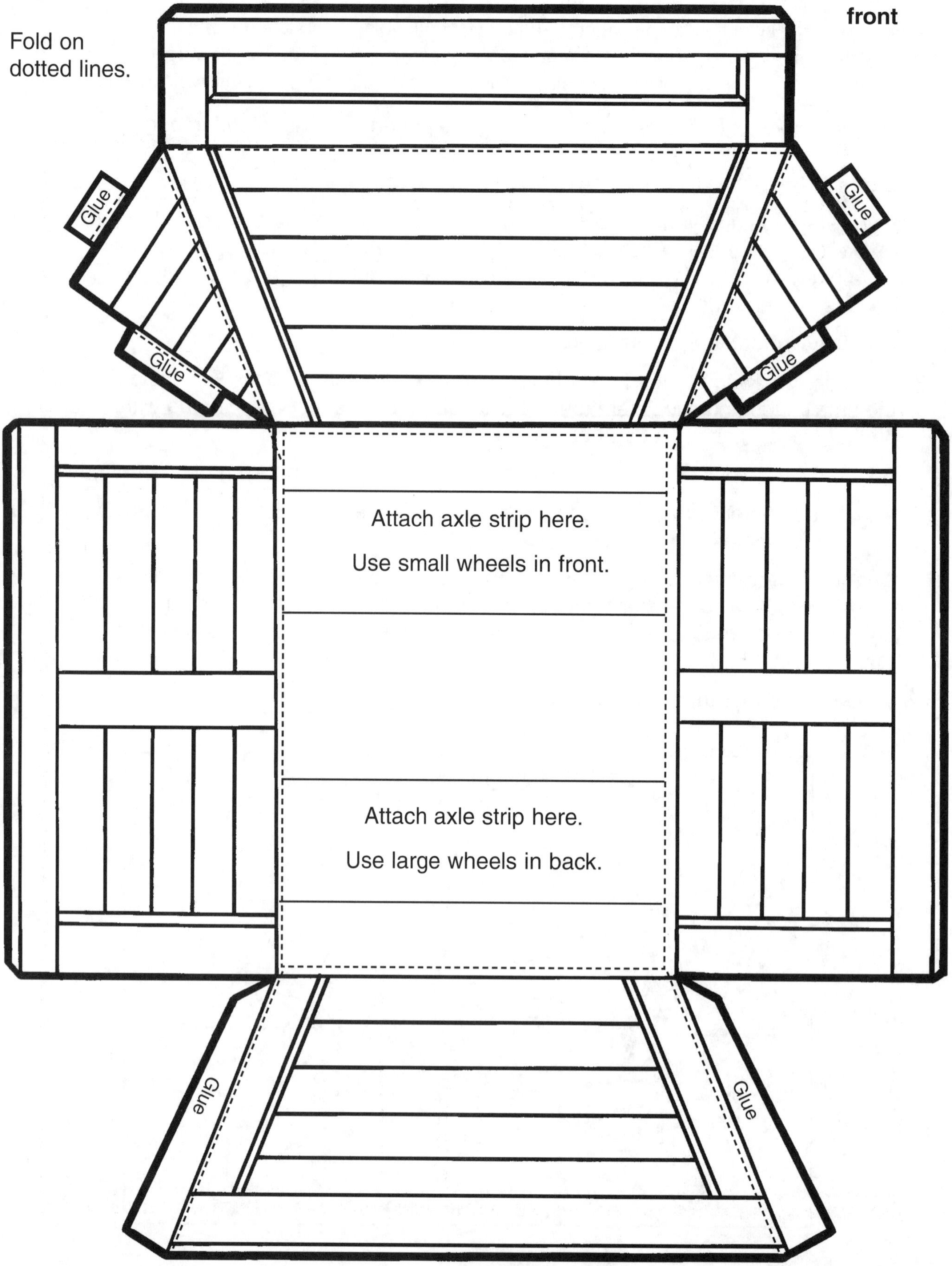

Glue

Glue

Glue

Glue

Attach axle strip here.

Use small wheels in front.

Attach axle strip here.

Use large wheels in back.

Glue

Glue

Chuck Wagon Templates *(cont.)*

wagon roof (Roll before attaching to wagon sides.)

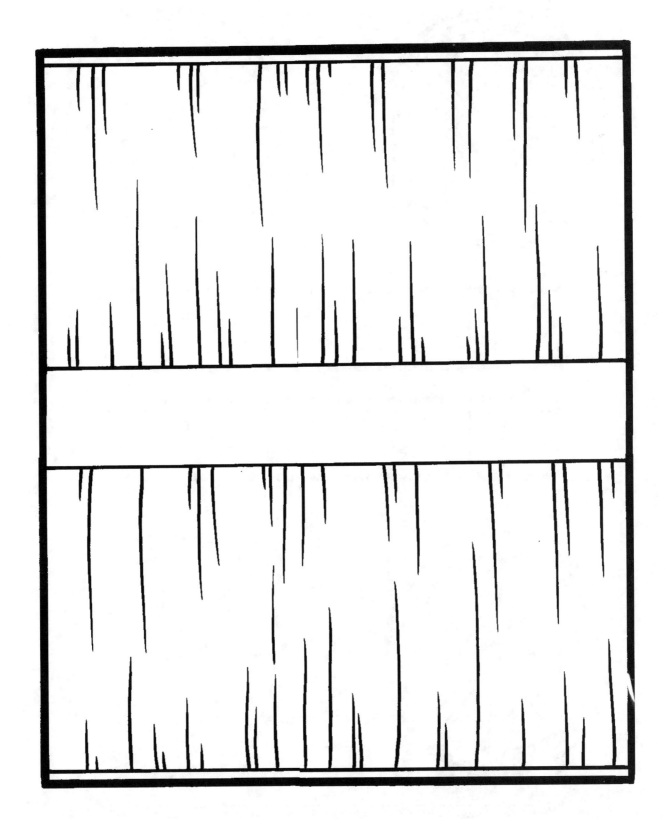

Chuck Wagon Templates *(cont.)*

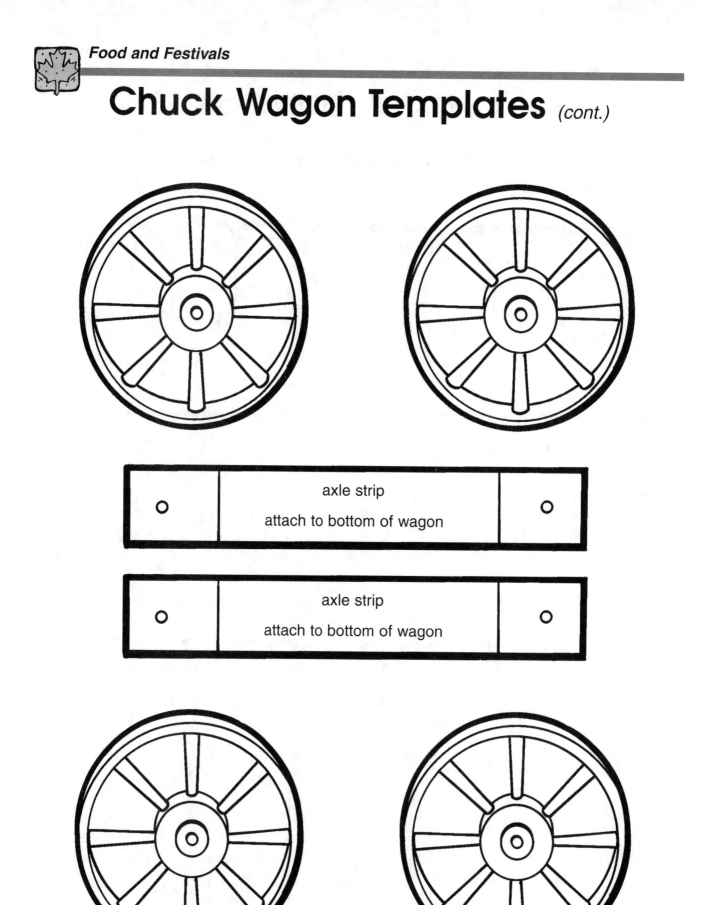

axle strip

attach to bottom of wagon

axle strip

attach to bottom of wagon

Chuck Wagon Stew

When trail cooks prepared dinner for the cowboys, they did not do a lot of fancy cooking. They often cooked the food all together in one pot. Stews were very popular. The cooks would use whatever they had on hand, and these tasty dishes combined everything for the meal in one hot dish.

You can make a simple stew for yourself by following these instructions. Be sure to have an adult help you with the cooking.

Ingredients and Equipment

- a piece of aluminum foil about 30 cm x 61 cm (12" x 24")
- 250 mL (1 cup) of ground beef or two cut-up hotdogs
- 1 small onion cut into small pieces
- 1 carrot cut into small pieces
- 1 small potato cut into small pieces
- some salt and pepper

Directions

Put all of the ingredients on the foil. If you use hotdogs, add a little bit of water to the ingredients. Pull the long edges up and fold them over about three times. Fold the short edges over about three times. Make sure that the food is completely sealed in and nothing can leak out.

You can put your foil dinner directly into the hot coals of a campfire or a fireplace and let it cook for about 15 minutes. You can also put your dinner into an oven at 177°C (350°F) for about 15 minutes. You can also set it on a gas or charcoal grill.

Have an adult help you take your dinner out of the fire or the oven with tongs. Try not to put holes in the foil. You will be able to hear the food cooking inside of the foil. Have an adult unfold the foil to see if the food is done.

Put your food on a plate and eat it with bread and butter. You will have a true pioneer dinner!

The Winter Carnival

How would you like to see a walking, talking snowman? Well, at the Winter Carnival in Quebec, the host is a giant, friendly snowman. His name is Bonhomme, which is French for "Good Man." Every year thousands of people come to Quebec to meet Bonhomme and share in the snowy fun of winter.

The world's largest winter festival is held for 17 days every year. From the end of January until the middle of February, the city of Quebec turns into a winter wonderland. Bonhomme's house is a huge ice castle and the city is decorated with hundreds of ice and snow sculptures. Strings of lights and happy music fill the air, along with the scent of great food and winter. The first winter carnival in Quebec was in 1894, but the celebration did not become a continuous, annual event until 1955. Since then, it is the third-largest pre-Lenten carnival in the world after the Carnaval of Rio de Janeiro and the Mardi Gras of New Orleans.

The central focus of the carnival is the famous palace made each year for Bonhomme. This castle is made of ice and has many rooms and even has electric lights inside. Every year the castle has a new and different design and of course, each year the designers attempt to surpass the year before. The castle looks like a magical fairy palace and is the center of activity for the entire festival.

Bonhomme roams around the carnival in his merry red hat and scarf, but other characters are there, too. The most famous of these are the Knuks. The Knuks were having trouble with their enemies, the Grrrounchs. Bonhomme happened along when the trouble was going on and he convinced the sides to become friendly and sign a peace treaty. The Knuks have left their homes at the North Pole every year to join in the Winter Carnival and to honor their friend, Bonhomme. The Knuks are very lively and playful and in their brightly-colored costumes, they represent the "joie de vivre" (jwa du viv [re]) of the festival. This is a French term for the "joy of living."

Maybe you can find out more about the Quebec winter carnival and tell your classmates what you learned. The official Web site for the carnival is at *http://www.carnaval.qc.ca*

Try it and read the story of Bonhomme and the Knuks.

Classroom Winter Carnival

You can have a winter carnival in your classroom. Here are some ideas!

Look on the Web site for the Quebec winter carnival to find out more about the events at the world's largest winter carnival. *http://www.carnaval.qc.ca*

If you live somewhere where the winters are cold and you have snow, then you are lucky! Choose a date in early February and plan your carnival. You will have to work fast so the snow won't melt.

Make a snow fort or palace for Bonhomme

Make a snowman to look like Bonhomme. Dress him in a red scarf and hat.

Plan some of the following winter activities:

- a sled race.
- an ice skating party.
- a snowball competition where you throw snowballs at targets.
- a "who can make the biggest snowball" competition.
- a creative sled competition where people make sleds out of unusual things.
- a winter decoration party.

Even if you live somewhere where there is no snow, you can still have a winter carnival.

Consider the following:

- Make a winter scene in your classroom using angel hair for snow.
- Make a Bonhomme for your bulletin board.
- Make a Bonhomme out of white balloons!
- Have a party where only white food is served. Use lots of coconut flakes to look like snow on cakes and cupcakes. Use lots of powdered sugar.
- Serve snow cones.
- Have a contest where you see who can keep a white balloon in the air the longest.
- Play winter music like "Winter Wonderland" and "Frosty the Snowman."

Have fun with winter! Above all else, don't forget the "joie de vivre"!

Ann's Igloo Cake

Ingredients

- cake mix
- white icing
- coconut

Directions

1. Buy a white cake mix and follow the directions. Instead of baking it in a regular cake pan, use a rounded metal bowl that has been coated with oil.

2. Save some of the batter to bake in a small, rectangular pan to make the entrance for the igloo. You can also use an empty metal can filled half full.

3. Bake the cake and the igloo door and let both parts cool. You will have to adjust the cooking time for the shapes of the pieces.

4. Place the cake on top of a piece of mirror with beveled or polished edges to be decorated.

5. Shape and attach the doorway onto the igloo with icing. Ice the rest of the cake, sprinkle with coconut for snow. Leave some icing and coconut on the mirror. If you have a figurine of an animal or Eskimo or can make one out of clay, do it to the proportions of the entrance. Try dyeing some of the icing blue. Use a toothpick to add the details of the ice blocks or more ice around the igloo.

Canadian Food

One thing that many Canadian children look forward to in the morning is a stack of pancakes with maple syrup. Since maple syrup is so popular in Canada, pancakes are a special treat. Try making your own pancakes with this quick and easy recipe. You can also use this recipe to make waffles in a waffle iron.

Pancakes

Materials

- 314 mL (1 1/3 cups) flour
- 15 mL (1 tbsp) sugar
- 10 mL (2 tsp) baking powder
- 2 eggs
- 236 mL (1 cup) milk

Directions

1. Mix the ingredients thoroughly but do not over mix.

2. Spoon your batter onto a hot griddle or skillet with just a little cooking oil or spray-on oil.

3. Let one side brown, then flip over to brown the other side.

4. Remove from the griddle and stack on plates.

5. Smother with maple syrup and serve while warm.

This recipe serves about 4 people. Make sure that the maple syrup is at room temperature when you pour it on the pancakes. Cold syrup will make your pancakes cold. If you use whole-wheat flower and brown sugar in place of the flour and sugar, you will have pancakes with more of a maple-like flavor.

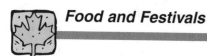
English Tea

Having afternoon tea is an old tradition in England. Many of the people of Canada adopted that tradition, and it is still practiced in hotels, restaurants, and some homes. Tea is usually served around 4:00 in the afternoon and dinner is served much later. A "High Tea" can be quite an extensive affair with sandwiches, biscuits (which are like cookies), and small cakes being served along with the tea. Tea can also be quite simple, with just tea and scones or biscuits.

Having afternoon tea can be a fun experience for students. You may want to select a caffeine-free tea for the children. The tea should be brewed in a pot so the children can have the experience of pouring the tea into teacups or mugs. Milk and sugar should be available for those who want it.

Set the tables with tablecloths, small plates, and teacups. Have the children make decorations for the tables or put flowers into small vases.

You might want to serve this as a side to the tea.

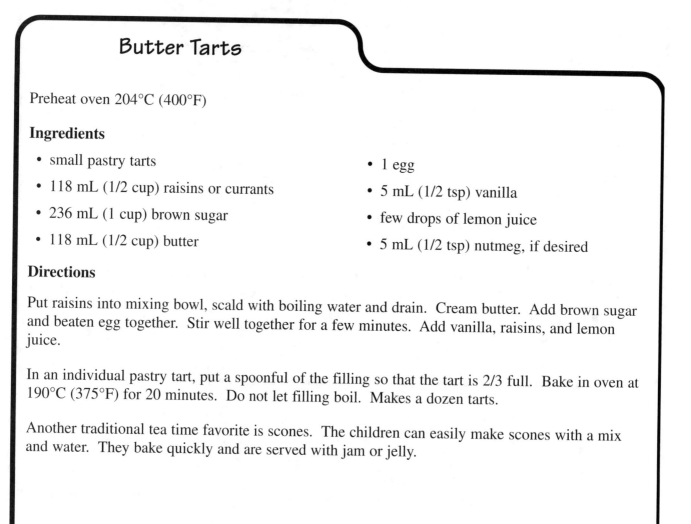

Butter Tarts

Preheat oven 204°C (400°F)

Ingredients

- small pastry tarts
- 118 mL (1/2 cup) raisins or currants
- 236 mL (1 cup) brown sugar
- 118 mL (1/2 cup) butter

- 1 egg
- 5 mL (1/2 tsp) vanilla
- few drops of lemon juice
- 5 mL (1/2 tsp) nutmeg, if desired

Directions

Put raisins into mixing bowl, scald with boiling water and drain. Cream butter. Add brown sugar and beaten egg together. Stir well together for a few minutes. Add vanilla, raisins, and lemon juice.

In an individual pastry tart, put a spoonful of the filling so that the tart is 2/3 full. Bake in oven at 190°C (375°F) for 20 minutes. Do not let filling boil. Makes a dozen tarts.

Another traditional tea time favorite is scones. The children can easily make scones with a mix and water. They bake quickly and are served with jam or jelly.

Christmas Pudding and Wedding Cakes

Fruitcakes and puddings are traditions that were brought to Canada from Great Britain. These desserts are heavier than what we usually have in the United States and use fruit for sweetness. Christmas cakes and wedding cakes are usually heavy fruitcakes.

Christmas cake is usually not iced whereas a wedding cake usually has a Marzipan layer then a Royal Icing on top with decorations. The decorations will last for a very long time. One friend has saved the decorations from her mother's cake for over 50 years and from her own for 23 years.

The wedding cakes are layered the same as wedding cakes in the United States. They can be different sizes with elaborate icing and decorations. Both cakes can be either a dark color or a light color and may be made well in advance and stored in airtight containers to "age."

At the wedding reception, one layer is usually already cut up in small pieces and wrapped in plastic wrap and ribbon. The couple then hands them out to their guests. Tradition has it if you put your piece under your pillow that night, you will dream about whom you will marry. The top layer is often saved to share at the baptism party for the couple's first-born child.

Mardy's Christmas Pudding

- 473 mL (2 cups) bread crumbs
- 236 mL (1 cup) brown sugar
- 355 mL (1 1/2 cup) suet
- 355 mL (1 1/2 cup) currants
- 355 mL (1 1/2 cup) raisins
- 118 mL (1/2 cup) mixed peel
- 236 mL (1 cup) chopped almonds

- 5 mL (1 tsp.) cinnamon
- 5 mL (1 tsp.) nutmeg
- 118 mL (1/2 tsp.) cloves
- 4 eggs
- 10 mL (2 tsp.) baking powder
- 10 mL (1 tsp.) salt
- some whole or halved candied cherries to taste

Directions

Mix the ingredients and put the mixture in a deep bowl. Securely cover the bowl with waxed paper and foil and secure it around the edges with string. Steam mixture in large saucepan and water for 4–8 hours. Store. Steam again for 2 hours before serving. It will be a rich dark color. Garnish with holly or spearmint leaves or cherries.

Christmas pudding is a delicious finish to the festive meal. It can be made ahead and stored in an airtight container. It has to be "steamed" to cook and then steamed again before serving. It can be served with whipped cream.

Christmas Pudding and Wedding Cakes *(cont.)*

Wegg's Christmas Fruitcake

Ingredients

- 236 mL (1 cup) white sugar
- 177 mL (3/4 cup) brown sugar
- 473 mL (2 cups) butter
- 1 L (4.5 cups) flour
- 20 mL (4 tsp.) baking powder
- 6 eggs (beaten)
- 236 mL (1 cup) citrus peel (orange or lemon)
- 10 mL (1 tsp.) almond extract

- 10 mL (1 tsp.) vanilla extract
- 900 g (2 pounds) light raisins– whole
- 900 g (2 pounds) almonds whole or chopped and skin free
- 450 g (1 pound) red cherry – half and some whole
- 450 g (1 pound) green cherry – half and some whole
- 450 g (1 pound) glazed pineapple – pieces
- 230 g (1/2 pound) brazil nuts (optional)

Directions

Heat oven to 163°C (325°F). Mix sugar, butter, and beaten eggs in a mixing bowl. Sift flour, baking powder, and salt together. Add the sugar mixture alternating with milk and flour. Add vanilla and almond extracts. Mix in fruit and nuts that have been lightly floured with some flour from the 1 L (4 1/2 cup) amount. Stir well. The mixture will be heavy and hard to turn over into the pan.

One tradition is to make a wish as you turn it into the pan. Have all of the participants join in for this fun tradition.

Preparation of the cooking pans is important. Line square pans with waxed or greased brown paper. Crease at corners of tin. No area should be bare of paper including bottom. Press mixture into pan 3/4 way up. Bake 2 to 2 1/2 hrs. Store well-sealed to age in a cool spot but do not refrigerate. You can make this in late October or November to be ready for Christmas. Be sure to seal the container tightly!

These desserts are more elaborate to make, but it will give the students a good idea about the wedding and Christmas traditions of Canada and Great Britain.

Quick and Easy Treats

This quick, easy recipe is fun for an outdoor activity.

Bannock (hot bread)

Ingredients

- 946 mL (4 cups) flour
- 5 mL (1 tsp.) salt
- 44 mL (3 tbsp.) baking powder
- raisins (optional)
- 29.5 mL (2 tbsp.) oil
- 355 mL (1 1/2 cups) water (more can be added if needed)

Directions

Mix dry ingredients in a mixing bowl. Slowly add oil and water, stirring with a wooden spoon. Put mixture on a floured counter and knead gently—don't over mix. Oil a large 23 cm x 30 cm (9" x 12") cake pan or cookie sheet. Place bannock in pan and then flip over so that both sides of mixture are oiled. Next, pull bannock into long thin strips and wrap around the end of a stick 13–15 cm (5–6"). Hold stick over coals of a fire until golden. Serve with margarine/butter and jam.

Optional: Buy bread dough in a roll or buy a bread dough mix.

Poutine

A really all-time favorite food in Quebec will be a hit with your students. It is a recipe that calls for three things: French fries, gravy, and cheese curd.

The recipe is simple. Put the cheese on the hot fries and cover with the gravy. Allow the cheese to melt and you have poutine. Notice that there is no specified gravy. Any kind will do, according to your taste. There are hundreds of kinds of poutine, including Italian poutine served with spaghetti sauce.

The type of French fries makes a difference, too. Curly fries, frozen fries, spicy fries. . . take your choice.

This dish is so popular in Canada that it is even served at McDonald's™!

Making Maple Sugar

The Native Americans introduced the new settlers to the taste of maple sugar. Since cane sugar from the West Indies was expensive, the new Canadians learned how to tap the maple trees for the sweet sap. However, the first thing that they learned was when to begin the harvest. Usually, this would happen in March when it was still cold at night and milder during the days.

First, they bored a hole in the tree. Next, they hammered a wooden spike into the tree. Then they placed a bucket under the spike to catch to sap. The bucket from the day's collection was taken to the boiling kettles via sleds. The children had the important task of gathering twigs to keep the big kettles of sap boiling. Eventually, the watery sap would turn into the thick sweet liquid, but someone would have to constantly stir the kettle to keep the syrup from burning. The containers to hold the syrup were made ready so that the syrup could be ladled into them. If solid sugar was needed, the kettles were kept cooking over a low fire. The brown maple sugar was packed in wooden boxes.

When the sugaring was done, the fun of scraping the kettles was next. If there was a nice blanket of snow, someone would spoon the syrup on top of the snow to make a sweet candy treat.

In the Quebec countryside, there are sugar shacks called "cabanes a sucre." There they serve up maple syrup in all kinds of ways. One maple syrup treat that is eaten in Canada is called "trempette." This easy-to-make dish is simple bread soaked in maple syrup and served with lots of fresh cream.

144

Life Without Grocery Stores

Since maple syrup and maple sugar were available in Canada, people used the sweet syrup to make desserts and treats. One example is Maple Syrup Pie. This pie has many variations, as the ingredients changed with availability.

This is a classic dessert of Quebec. The smooth, rich filling is usually shallow and very sweet. This is still popular in Quebec, but there are variations throughout Canada. Molasses was often used when ingredients were scarce. Maple syrup, maple sugar, and brown sugar can all be used for this recipe.

Maple Syrup Pie (1 serving)

Ingredients

- 118 mL (½ cup) cold water
- 1 egg, lightly beaten
- 59 mL (¼ cup) all purpose flour
- 29.5 mL (2 tb.) butter
- 236 mL (1 cup) maple syrup
- an 20 cm (8") pie shell

Directions

Whisk water with flour until smooth; stir into syrup in small, heavy saucepan. Stir in the egg and cook over medium or low heat, stirring until thick—about 7 minutes. Stir in butter until melted. Pour into pie shell. Let cool.

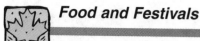

Life Without Grocery Stores *(cont.)*

This is a favorite in the Yukon. People of different areas eat the food that is available to them. This is a common dish in the Yukon and the Northwest.

Salmon Patties

Ingredients

- 450 g (16 oz.) can pink salmon, bones and skin removed (reserve liquid)
- 2 beaten eggs
- 118 mL (1/2 cup) chopped onion
- 30 mL (2 tbsp.) butter

- 236 mL (1 cup) dry bread crumbs
- 5 mL (1 tsp.) dried dill weed
- 2.5 mL (1/2 tsp.) dried mustard
- 30 mL (2 tbsp.) cooking oil

Directions

Drain salmon, reserving the liquid. Sauté onion in butter until tender. Remove from heat. Add salmon liquid, 118 mL (1/2 cup) of the bread crumbs, eggs, dill weed, mustard, and salmon. Mix well and shape into four patties, then coat with remaining crumbs. Heat oil in a skillet and cook patties over medium heat about three minutes on each side or until nicely browned.

Enjoy this treat while you read *The Polar Bear Son* or while you wear your snow goggles.

Life Without Grocery Stores *(cont.)*

In the Maritime Provinces where there are deep, cool forests, one delicacy they enjoy is Fiddlehead ferns. Cooking the young fern shoots makes a green treat after a long, snowy winter without fresh vegetables.

The sea supplies more than fish for food. Have you ever heard of dulse? Dulse is a sea vegetable, which takes root on rocks. It is gathered and dried in the sun for six hours. It can be eaten like potato chips, toasted, or added to salads or soups. It is found on Grand Manan Island in New Brunswick from June to October.

Sea Weed Chowder

Ingredients

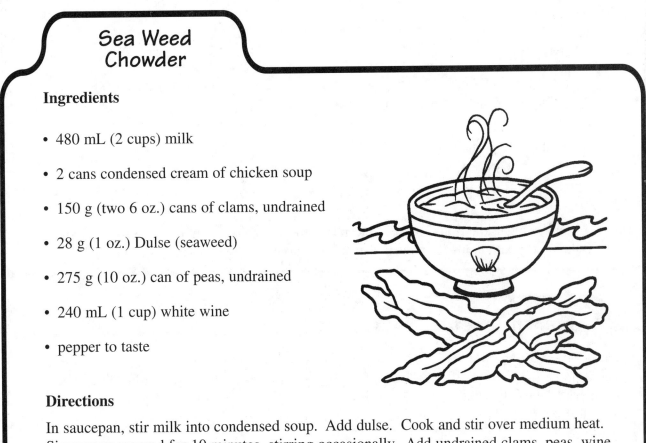

- 480 mL (2 cups) milk

- 2 cans condensed cream of chicken soup

- 150 g (two 6 oz.) cans of clams, undrained

- 28 g (1 oz.) Dulse (seaweed)

- 275 g (10 oz.) can of peas, undrained

- 240 mL (1 cup) white wine

- pepper to taste

Directions

In saucepan, stir milk into condensed soup. Add dulse. Cook and stir over medium heat. Simmer uncovered for 10 minutes, stirring occasionally. Add undrained clams, peas, wine, and pepper. Simmer 5 more minutes and serve. Serves 8.

Toasted Dulse

Place a handful of whole-leaf dulse on a paper plate. Place in microwave for 45 seconds. Great treat!

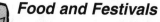

Life Without Grocery Stores *(cont.)*

Of course two of the favorite foods of Canada are maple sugar and maple syrup. It was a natural food source that meant a lot to the native people and to the settlers who came to the area. Using the sweet sugar and syrup made many foods pleasant and enjoyable.

Try making these sweet treats in the classroom.

Tarte au Sucre (Sugar Pie)

Preheat oven 204 °C (400 °F)

Ingredients

- 118 mL (1/2 cup) maple sugar
- 118 mL (1/2 cup) brown sugar
- 30 mL (2 tbsp.) flour
- 1 unbaked pie shell
- 118 mL (1/2 cup) whipping cream

Directions

Combine sugar and flour. Spread into pie shell. Pour the cream over the mixture and bake until golden (30–40 minutes depending on your oven). Serve warm. Yum!

French Toast

This is a quick, easy treat that can be made in an electric skillet or on a griddle in the classroom. Fun for a class breakfast!

Ingredients

- French bread
- eggs
- maple syrup
- butter
- cooking oil

Directions

Choose a loaf of French bread and slice it into 2.54 cm (1") slices. Spray a skillet lightly with oil and begin heating it. Stir your eggs in a shallow bowl. You will need about 1 egg for every 3 slices of bread. Dip each slice of bread in the beaten eggs. Put slices onto the hot skillet. Cook toast until golden on each side. Serve with butter and maple syrup.

148

Storing Food

Another consideration in the old days was preserving food. The people had to use everything they had, but they did not have refrigeration or canning to keep food for long periods of time. Since people relied largely on hunting, it was important not to waste any of the meat. There were several methods for keeping meat. Smoking, salting and drying were the most common ways. Native Americans shared their knowledge with early pioneers and taught them how to preserve their meats.

Two ways of keeping meat were to make jerky or to make pemmican. Here are methods for these types of meat preservation.

Jerky

Jerky is simply dried strips of meat. After a successful hunt, the hunters would cut the meat into thins strips. They would then put the meat in the smoke of a hardwood fire to give it a good taste. Then they would let the meat dry in the sun for 4 to 6 hours. It was easy to carry the dried meat in saddlebags and packs. If you would like to try jerky today, it is easy to find packages of jerky in convenience stores and sporting goods stores.

Pemmican

Pemmican has been made by many North American people for thousands of years. It was a way of storing the meat of a hunt for a future time of hunger. It was very important to the survival of a tribe that everything from the hunt was used from the animal. Preserving food was a community effort in order to save every possible bit for times when hunting was poor.

Pemmican was easily carried, didn't spoil, and it provided protein, vitamins from the berries, and energy from the fat. Second to the fur trade, the making of pemmican was a very important industry, not only from a financial standpoint, but also from a survival one. The Métis Indians would prepare pemmican after a bison hunt, and they would supply fur traders and trappers with this important product.

Pemmican was made by mixing jerky with other nutritious things like berries and nuts. The cooks would pound jerky into a powder by pounding it with a stone. Then the meat would be mixed with lard or bone marrow grease, nuts, seeds and dried berries. This "dough" would be rolled into balls and carried along in packs.

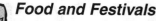
Storing Food *(cont.)*

Salting meat was another way of preserving it without refrigeration. Voyageurs who traveled from Montreal were known as "porkeaters" because they ate a lot of salted pork on their travels. These fur traders had relatively plain food while on their trips, but once they reached their rendezvous, game and special foods brought by the Europeans were provided to reward those who had made the long journey.

Here is a favorite known to many Canadians, especially those in Quebec where it's very popular.

Nikki's Tourtiere

Before you start cooking, preheat oven to 425°F (218°C)

Ingredients (combine in a saucepan)

- 675 g (1 1/2 lbs). pork
- 236 mL (1 cup) finely chopped onion
- 118 mL (1/2 cup) water
- 1 bay leaf
- 7 mL (1 1/2 tsp.) salt

- 5 mL (1/2 tsp.) thyme
- 1 mL (1/4 tsp.) cloves
- 1 mL (1/4 tsp.) pepper
- pastry shell

Directions

Bring water to boil, add pork, and cook until it loses red color, stirring constantly. Then grind the pork. Add the other ingredients. Cover, reduce heat, and simmer for about 45 minutes or until very tender. Remove bay leaf. While meat mixture is cooking, make the pastry shell. Roll out half of pastry and line a 9-inch pie plate. Fill with meat mixture and cover with top crust madefrom remaining pastry. Seal and flute edges. Slash top. Bake in oven for 15 minutes or until golden. Then reduce heat to 350°F (176°C) and bake for an additional 15 to 20 minutes. Serve with tomato catsup (optional). Makes six servings.

Meat pies are very popular in Great Britain and came to Canada from the British immigrants.

Storing Food (cont.)

Another favorite meat dinner in the French Canadian areas is this one.

Bastian's Bouilli Canadien (boiled dinner)

Ingredients

In a large 0.7 kg (1 1/2 lb.) beef brisket, add the following:

- 225 g (1/2 lb.) salt pork or ham
- 2.5 mL (1/2 tsp.) pepper
- 1 bay leaf
- 3 whole cloves
- 710 mL (3 cups) water

Directions

Bring to a boil, cover, reduce heat, and simmer for about 4 hours or until meat is almost tender. Then add the following:

- 6 carrots
- 6 onions
- 1/2 turnip, sliced into 6 portions
- 1 stalk celery, cut into 6

Continue cooking for 15 additional minutes and then add the following:

- 1 cabbage, sliced into 6 portions
- 225 g (1/2 lb.) green beans

Cook for 15 minutes longer and then remove cloves and bay leaf. Traditionally this is served in soup bowls with meat, vegetables, and broth. If desired, serve broth separately as soup and then in a main course of meat and vegetables. Makes six servings.

Government

A Distinctive Flag for Canada

For many years, Canada did not have its own official flag. The flag that was used in Canada was often the British flag. In 1913 Canada gained its independence from Great Britain, but it still did not have its own official flag. Everyone argued whether Canada should have its own distinctive flag or use the British flag as part of theirs.

In 1964 the Canadian Parliament decided to create an official flag. There was much discussion and debate about what the flag should look like. Finally George F. G. Stanley designed the flag. He chose a red maple leaf on a white square surrounded by two bands of red. Why were these symbols chosen for the flag?

The maple leaf has been a symbol of Canada since the early 1800s. Canada has many maple trees and the trees have been used for maple syrup, maple sugar, fuel, and making things throughout the history of the country. The maple leaf on the flag was carefully designed so that it would look nice when the flag flutters in the wind.

Red and white have been the official colors of Canada since 1921 when the Canadian coat of arms was created.

In the end, George F. G. Stanley designed a very distinctive flag for Canada. It has a very different look from other flags of the world, and it is easily recognizable as the flag of Canada.

The flag is called the Maple Leaf Flag. On January 28, 1965, Queen Elizabeth II of England proclaimed it to be the official flag of Canada. The flag was raised for the first time on February 15, 1965, and flew on a staff just east of the Peace Tower in Ottawa.

The Canadian flag may be displayed from government buildings from sunrise to sunset. In Canada they also display the flag on the following holidays:

- New Year's Day, January 1
- Good Friday (no fixed date)
- Easter Monday (no fixed date)
- Victoria Day and the Queen's Birthday, the Monday before May 25
- Canada Day, July 1
- Labour Day, the first Monday in September
- Thanksgiving Day, the second Monday in October
- Remembrance Day, November 11
- Christmas Day, December 25

Think About It

Which of these holidays is celebrated in the United States? On what days do we fly our flag? Why do countries have flags?

Canadian Flag

O Canada!—The Canadian National Anthem

Canada is a nation of two languages. Many people in Quebec and in New Brunswick speak French. Some people throughout other parts of Canada speak French, too.

When you go to the stores in Canada, you may see cans and boxes with French and English both printed on them. Some of the road signs have both languages.

English

O Canada!
    Our home and native land!
True patriot love
    in all thy sons command.
With glowing hearts
    we see thee rise,
The True North
    strong and free!
From far and wide,
    O Canada,
We stand on guard
    for thee.
God keep our land
    glorious and free!
O Canada,
    we stand on guard for thee.
O Canada,
    we stand on guard for thee!

French

Ô Canada
    Terre de nos aïeux,
Ton front est ceint
    de fleurons glorieux!
Car ton bras
    sait porter l'ëpée,
Il sait porter
    la croix!
Ton histoire
    est une épopée
Des plus
    brillants exploits,
Et ta valeur,
    de foi trempée,
Protégera nos foyers
    et nos droits,
Protégera nos foyers
    et nos droits.

Heraldry

Each province of Canada has a crest that represents it. The crest is used on flags and on official papers and documents. The crest has symbols on it that represent the province. Using these symbols and the crests is called *heraldry*.

Heraldry is a tradition that started in Europe about 1100 A.D. Important and powerful families would design a shield or crest to identify their homes, land, and belongings. The tradition became very widely used, and many people today have family crests or coats of arms.

The important thing about the crests is the symbolism that is used. Look at the crest of a province and try to decide why that province chose those symbols to represent it.

Why would there be a lion or a sheaf of wheat on a crest? Why would a crest have a boat or mountains?

Each symbol has a particular meaning. Here are some examples.

Lions show power and strength. Lions are also used frequently in the heraldry of England.

A sheaf of wheat indicates that the area grows crops and is prosperous.

A boat shows that the area is near water and depends on the sea for some of its livelihood.

The *fleur-de-lis* is a symbol often used in French heraldry. Why would we see it in the Canadian crests?

The basic shape of the shield is called the *escutcheon*. A picture on the escutcheon, like the lion, the boat, or the sheaf of wheat is called a *charge*. Most crests have more than one charge.

Choose one of the provincial crests and color it. Explain why the crest has the charges that it does.

On the next page, design a crest for yourself. What would you use to symbolize yourself? How would you like to present yourself to others? Display your crest in the classroom.

Bonus Activity: Try designing a crest for your school. Have a contest in your class to see who can create the best design.

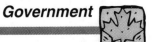

My Personal Crest

My name:_____

This is what my crest looks like.

The reason I chose these colors is

_____

_____

_____

_____

The reason I chose these symbols is

_____

_____

_____

_____

Provincial Seals and Information

The following pages contain basic information about each province and territory. On each page is the official seal for that province or territory. These pages are intended to provide background information that can be used in several different ways.

Use the pages for references for reports.

Have the students color the seals and explain the meanings of the colors and symbols. (See the information in the "Heraldry.")

Enlarge the crests and have the students color them.

Use the pages as cover pages for reports or to make a bulletin board display.

Divide the room into provinces and territories. Assign each student or group of students an area to research. Have them create a group report, book, bulletin board display or other presentation for the class.

Have students research the flags of the provinces. Have them compare the flags with the seals. What differences do they find? What similarities? Reinforce the skills of comparing and contrasting.

Have students recreate the flags on paper or fabric. Have a parade where the students can carry their flags and tell about the symbolism and the province.

Enlarge the seals and make stencils of the seal elements (lion, wheat sheaf, boat, etc.). Let the students trace the seal elements onto construction paper. The students can cut out the figures and paste them to a shield shape to make a provincial shield or create one of their own.

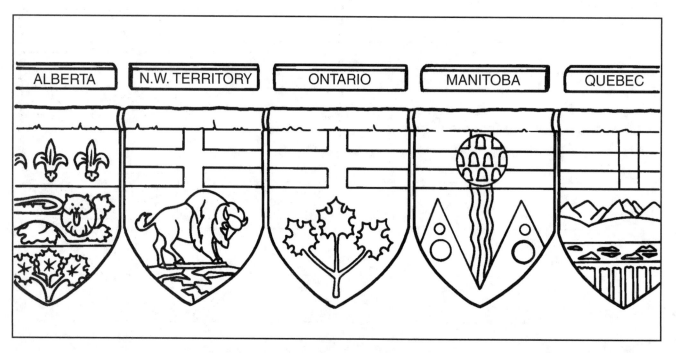

ALBERTA   N.W. TERRITORY   ONTARIO   MANITOBA   QUEBEC

Facts About Alberta

Population (2001 census): 2,974,807

Area: 661,185 square kilometers (255,285 square miles); rank – 4th province in size

Greatest Length (north to south): 1,220 kilometers (760 miles)

Greatest Width (east to west): 640 kilometers (400 miles)

Highest Elevation: Mountain Columbia, 3,747 meters (12,294 feet)

Largest Cities (2001 census)

- Calgary (city 878,866; metropolitan area, 951,395): manufacturing and agriculture center in wheat-growing and livestock-raising district; oil refining; meat-packing; flour milling; brewing; lumbering; site of famous annual rodeo

- Edmonton (city 666,104; metropolitan area 937,845): provincial capital; manufacturing and trading center in agricultural region; center of Canadian oil and natural gas development; coal mining

- Lethbridge (67,374): city in partly irrigated farm area; ranching; flour, beet sugar, coal; food processing.

Major Products

Agricultural: wheat, rapeseed, barley, cattle, hogs, timber

Manufactured: meat and poultry products, refined petroleum, chemicals, paper, wood products

Mined: crude petroleum, natural gas, sulfur, coal

Facts About Saskatchewan

Population (2001 census): 978,933

Area: 651,900 square kilometers (251,700 square miles); rank – 5th province in size

Highest Elevation: Cypress Hill, 1,386 meters (4,546 feet)

Largest Cities (2001 census)

- Saskatoon (city 196,811; metropolitan area 225,927): on Saskatchewan River; service, distributing, farming, and manufacturing center; University of Saskatchewan

- Regina (178,225): provincial capital; commercial and financial center; headquarters of Saskatchewan Wheat Pool, world's largest grain cooperative; Royal Canadian Mounted Police training facilities; University of Regina

Major Products

Agricultural: wheat, barley, oats, rapeseed, rye, flaxseed, canola

Manufactured: meat-packing, food processing, petroleum refining, printing, and publishing

Mined: petroleum, potash, uranium, coal, natural gas, copper, zinc.

Facts About Quebec

Population (2001 census): 7,237,479

Area: 1,540,680 square kilometers (594,860 square miles); rank – 1st province in size

Greatest Length (north to south): 1,971 kilometers (1,225 miles)

Greatest Width (east to west): 1,580 kilometers (982 miles)

Highest Elevation: Mount Jacques Cartier 1,268 meters (4,160 feet)

Largest Cities (2001 census)

- Montreal (3,426,350) largest city and chief seaport; industrial, financial, commercial and cultural center
- Laval (343,005): northwest of Montreal; city includes entire island of Ile-Jesus.
- Quebec (682,757): provincial capital; French Canadian cultural center; seaport; tourist center; diversified industry
- Longueuil (128,016): suburb of Montreal on east shore of St. Lawrence River

Major Products

Agriculture: trees, dairy cattle, poultry, soybeans

Manufactured: food and beverages, refined petroleum, paper and pulp, primary metals, transportation equipment, chemicals, metal products, clothing, and textiles

Mined: petroleum, natural gas, copper, coal, gold, iron ore, zinc, nickel, uranium, cement, potash, silver

Facts About Prince Edward Island

Population (2001 census): 135,294

Area: 5,659 square kilometers (2,185 square miles); rank – 10th province in size

Greatest Length (east to west): about 193 kilometers (120 miles)

Greatest Width (north to south): 55 kilometers (34 miles)

Highest Elevation: central Queens County, 142 meters (465 feet)

Largest Cities (2001 census)

- Charlottetown (32,245): provincial capital and only city, laid out in 1768; excellent harbor, commercial center, fishing, potato growing, dairying, meat-packing; Government House, home of lieutenant-governor; Province House; Confederation Center of the Arts; St. Peter's Anglican Cathedral; University of Prince Edward Island

- Summerside (14,654): on Bedeque Bay; Canadian Armed Forces air base nearby; oysters; lobster packing; sport fishing; farm center and agricultural products processing; woodworking.

Major Products

Agricultural: potatoes, tobacco, Irish moss, cattle, pigs, lobsters, scallops, oysters, tuna

Manufactured: fish products, dairy products, foods, wood products

Mined: sand and gravel, stone

Facts About Ontario

Population (2001 census): 11,410,046

Area: 1,068,582 square kilometers (412,582 square miles); rank – 2nd province in size

Greatest Length (north to south): 1,690 kilometers (1,050 miles)

Greatest Width (east to west): about 1,600 kilometers (1,000 miles)

Highest Elevation: Ogidaki Mountain 665 meters (2,183 feet)

Largest Cities (2001 census)

- Toronto (4,682,897): second largest city of Canada; provincial capital; commercial, financial, industrial, and educational center; provincial parliament buildings; CN Tower

- Hamilton (662,401): lake port; rail, steel, and diversified industrial center; Royal Botanical Gardens

- Ottawa (806,096): federal capital; papermaking, woodworking, publishing, federal Parliament Buildings

- London (432,451): commercial, educational, industrial and agricultural center

Major Products

Agricultural: corn, vegetables, soybeans, wheat, tobacco, potatoes, cattle, dairy products, pigs

Manufactured: automobiles, iron and steel, machinery, commercial and industrial equipment, pulp and paper, publishing and printing, refined petroleum, food and beverages, plastics, chemicals

Mined: nickel, uranium, silver, copper, gold, iron ore, gypsum, salt, cement, clay products, lime, sand and gravel, stone

Facts About Nova Scotia

Population (2001 census): 908,007

Area: 55,490 square kilometers (21,425 square miles); rank – 9th province in size

Greatest Length (north to south): 613 kilometers (381 miles)

Greatest Width (east to west): 241 kilometers (150 miles)

Highest Elevation: in Cape Breton Highlands National Park 532 meters (1,747 feet)

Largest Cities (2001 census)

- Halifax (359,183): provincial capital and largest city
- Cape Breton (109,330)

Major Products

Agricultural: dairy products, eggs, poultry, fruits, vegetables, beef, pigs

Manufactured: fish products, publishing, ships, wood products, food and beverages, animal feed, tires

Mined: coal, gypsum, barite, salt, peat, sand and gravel, petroleum, natural gas.

Facts About Newfoundland and abrador

Population (2001 census): 512,930

Area: 404,517 square kilometers (156,185 square miles); island 112,299 square kilometers (43,359 square miles) including 5,685 square kilometers (2,195 square miles) of water surface; Labrador 292,218 square kilometers (112,826 square miles), including 28,347 square kilometers (10,945 square miles) of water surface; rank – 7th province in size

Highest Elevation: Cirque Mountain 1,573 meters (5,160 feet) on Labrador and Lewis Hills 815 meters (2,673 feet) on island

Largest Cities (2001 census)

- St. John's (172,918): provincial capital; seaport and center for large fishing fleet; Memorial University of Newfoundland; food products, machinery, veneer, plywood, nets and cordage, electrical products

- Mount Pearl (24,964): residential town near St. John's Corner Brook (22,410). In lumbering region; pulp and paper mill; cement and gypsum plants; shipping center

- Gander (11,254): international airport; transportation center

Major Products

Agricultural: blueberries, potatoes, turnips, cabbage, eggs, dairy and beef cattle, pigs, chickens

Manufactured: fresh and salted fish, pulp and paper, particle board, lumber, food and beverages, boats, doors and windows, home crafts

Mined: iron, asbestos, zinc, limestone, gypsum, clay, shale, natural gas, petroleum

Facts About New Brunswick

Population (2001 census): 729,498

Area: 73,437 square kilometers (28,354 square miles); rank – 8th province in size

Highest Elevation: Mount Carleton 820 meters (2,690 feet)

Largest Cities (2001 census)

- Saint John (69,661; metropolitan area 122,678): manufacturing and commercial center

- Moncton (61,046): industrial and commercial city; rail and air center; port; food processing; woodworking; auto parts

- Fredericton (47,560): provincial capital; built on site of St. Anne's Point, old French village; boots and shoes, canoes, lumber and wood products; plastics

Major Products

Agricultural: potatoes, poultry, eggs, milk, pigs, beef cattle, apples, blueberries, strawberries, grain

Manufactured: food and beverages, pulp and paper, forestry products, furniture, fabricated metal products, printing and publishing, transportation equipment

Mined: antimony, lead, copper, zinc, bismuth, silver, gypsum, gold, peat, quartz, salt, coal, natural gas, petroleum, clay products, cement, line, sand, gravel, stone, potash

Facts About Manitoba

Population (2001 census): 1,119,583

Area: 649,950 square kilometers (250,947 square miles); rank – 6th province in size

Greatest Length (north to south): 1,223 kilometers (760 miles)

Greatest Width (east to west): 797 kilometers (495 miles)

Highest Elevation: Baldy Mountain 832 meters (2,729 feet)

Largest Cities (2001 census)

- Winnipeg (619,544): provincial capital; major cultural, commercial, and financial center; transportation center, grain market; flour, meat and food products; farm machinery and automobile manufacturing; railroad yards

- Brandon (39,716): on the Assiniboine River, distribution center for grain region; flour, meat, fertilizer, chemicals and petroleum processing

- Thompson (13,256): largest city in northern Manitoba; nickel mining

Major Products

Agricultural: wheat, barley, rapeseed, hay, cattle, pigs, dairy products

Manufactured: food and beverages, machinery, primary metal fabrication, printing and publishing, clothing, pulp and paper, refined petroleum, computers, and fiber optics

Mined: nickel, copper, zinc

Facts About British Columbia

Population (2001 census): 3,907,738

Area: 948,596 square kilometers (366,255 square miles); rank: 3rd province in size

Greatest Length (north to south): 1,300 kilometers (800 miles)

Greatest Width (east to west): 1,060 kilometers (660 miles)

Highest Elevation: Mount Fairweather 4,663 meters (15,300 feet)

Largest Cities (2001 census)

- Vancouver (545,671; metropolitan area 1,986,965): Provincial capital; 19th century British architecture and atmosphere; shipbuilding; connected to mainland by ferry; resort city with scenic drives and beautiful gardens

- Prince George (72,406): at confluence of Nechako and Fraser rivers; lumbering and forest products industries; transportation hub; hunting and fishing

Major Products

Agricultural: cattle, tree fruit, wheat, fish (mainly salmon), timber.

Manufactured: lumber and plywood, pulp and paper, food and beverages

Mined: copper, natural gas, coal, molybdenum, crude petroleum

Facts About the Northwest Territories

Population (2001 census): 37,360; rank – 11th

Area: 3,426,320 square kilometers (1,322,902 square miles)

Highest Elevation: Mount Sir James MacBrien 2,762 meters (9,062 feet)

Largest Cities (2001 census)

- Yellowknife (16,541): territorial capital
- Hay River (3,510)
- Inuvik (2,894)

Major Products

Agricultural: vegetables, chickens, eggs, buffalo, beef cattle

Manufactured: petroleum products, food products, wood products, printed materials, soapstone, sculptures, embroidered clothing, paintings, prints

Mined: oil, natural gas, gold, zinc, lead, nickel, copper, silver, tungsten, diamonds

Facts About the Yukon

Population (2001 census): 28,674

Area: 483,450 square kilometers (185,550 square miles); rank – 9th

Highest Elevation: Mount Logan 5,959 meters (19,550 feet)

Largest Cities

- territorial capital: Whitehorse (19,058)
- Faro (313)

Major Products

Agricultural: hay, oats, wheat, barley, potatoes, cabbage, bean sprouts, honey, elk, bison, musk oxen

Manufactured: lumber and wood products, printed materials, food products, clothing

Mined: asbestos, coal, copper, gold, lead, nickel, silver, zinc, molybdenum

Facts About Nunavut

The newest Canadian territory, Nunavut came into being on April 1, 1999. Nunavut is the third territory in Canada, and it is the largest. This territory is farther north than any other populated area on earth.

Nunavut means "Our Land" in Inukitut, the language of the Inuit people.

The capital of Nunavut is Iqaluit. This town used to be known as Frobisher Bay before Nunavut became a separate territory from the Northwestern Territory.

One very interesting thing about Nunavut is that its Parliament Building in the capital is made entirely of ice. The building is constructed of large ice blocks from all over the territory, and uses traditional Inuit building techniques. For more information check out *http://www.thetoque.net/102301/nunavut.htm*

Nunavut is the homeland of the Inuit people. It covers a very large area, but only 26,000 people live in the territory.

Population (2001 census): 26,745

Total Area: 808,182 sq. mi. (2,093,190 sq. km.)

Land: 747,532 sq. mi. (1,936,113 sq. km.)

Fresh water: 60,648 sq. mi. (157,077 sq. km.)

The natural resources of Nunavut are oil, wildlife, water, and mining.

Strengths: Nunavut is encouraging tourism for those who want to see an unspoiled part of the world. The artwork of the Inuit people is attracting much attention. Nunavut has the spirit of a new land, eager to grow and become part of the world economy.

My Provincial Report

My name: _____

My province: _____

Capital: _____

Population: _____

Natural resources: _____

_____

It became a province of Canada in _____.

The flag of my province looks like this:

The colors on the flag represent: _____

_____

_____

The symbols on the flag represent: _____

_____

_____

The words mean: _____

_____

172

Provincial Fair and Awards

The Provincial Fair

The Provincial Fair is an activity that gives your students the opportunity to display their achievements during their study of Canada. The Provincial Fair should be presented in a festive manner. It can be a day-long activity or just part of a day. Here are some suggestions for the Provincial Fair.

1. Have students select provinces that they are interested in representing. Each province should be represented. These students will be responsible for planning the activity or activities that will share their knowledge at the fair.

2. Each province should have a table or area to display the information they have collected and created.

3. Have students demonstrate a craft from the province.

4. Students can make food or bring in food for other fair goers to try.

5. Students can display the seal for their province on the table or area they are using.

6. Students can begin the fair by singing the Canadian National Anthem.

7. Hang Canadian flags around the room and have one student tell about the flag's history.

8. Make maple leaf bookmarks or notecards to hand out at the fair.

9. Have students wear their moccasins to the fair.

10. Make sure that someone has made a large map of Canada with all of the provinces clearly marked.

11. Be sure to display crafts that the students have made while studying about Canada: Chilkat blankets, soap sculptures, totem poles, Arctic dioramas, masks, etc.

12. Have a chuck wagon race during the fair. Mark off an oval track on the floor with tape. Have students race their wagons around the track. The winner gets a prize.

13. Have a students dress as a cowboy and explain what each item of clothing is for.

14. Hand out Honorary Canadian Citizen Award and/or Maple Leaf Awards to students during the fair.

15. Have students write the tourist boards of their province to receive extra information in the mail. Students love to get the colorful brochures from the tourist offices. Addresses for the tourist bureaus are available online.

Maple Leaf Award

This award is presented to

_____

for being a good student in our class!

Good students do these things:

follow class rules

help others

have a cheerful attitude

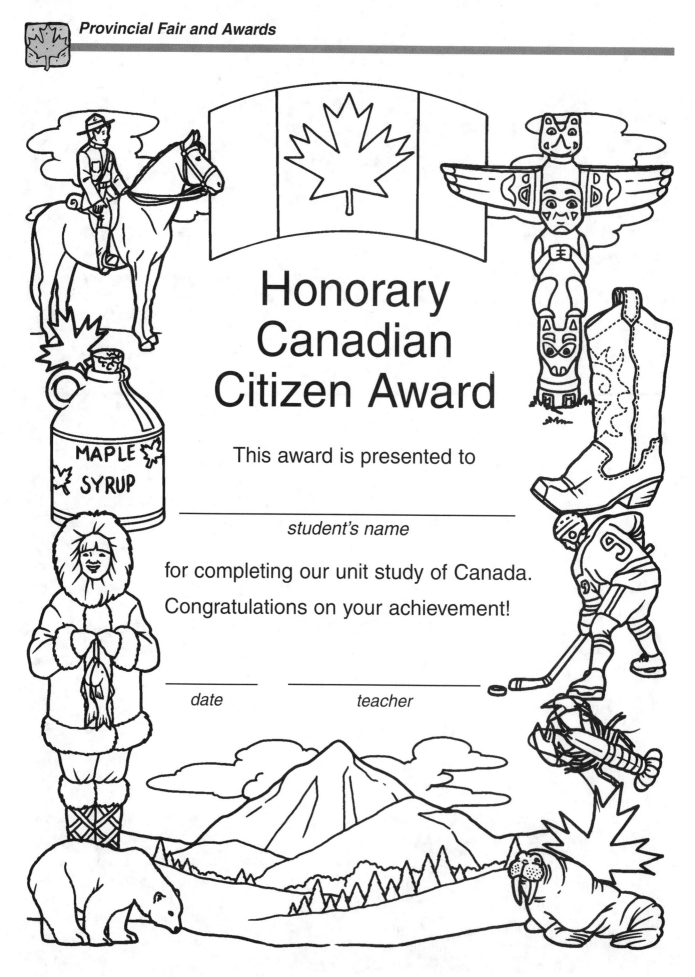

Honorary Canadian Citizen Award

This award is presented to

_____

student's name

for completing our unit study of Canada.
Congratulations on your achievement!

_____   _____

date   *teacher*